Starting Out

Preparing Yourselves for Marriage

First published 2020.

Second edition June 2020

For further details about Sozo for Couples visit www.sozoforcouples.org

Contact answers@sozoforcouples.org

The Sozo for Couples manual is available on Amazon.

'Wonderfully Free…no going back' the 31-day post-Sozo devotional journal is also available on Amazon. Details at www.wonderfullyfree.org.

Thanks

To Robin Henderson for his continued support of the Sozo for Couples ministry; Margaret Baird for her proof reading and suggestions; Dr. Fergus Law for the wisdom and clarity of his editing, and to those brave friends who added comments and whose joint efforts have made all the difference. Good job, guys!

Dedication

To Anthea and Stuart

Contents

Foreword

Our hope and desire as you read through this book is that it will give you strong foundations on which to build a long and healthy marriage. You'll be investing in your future together. That's what Liz and Stuart did. They invested by spending time preparing for their marriage. At the time they found the preparation helpful but the truth is that it was only years later, when they faced a challenging situation in their marriage, that they experienced the true benefit of having spent that time preparing and discussing things. In that situation, during those moments of high emotion, with thoughts and feelings whirling around them, knowing and having previously prepared a plan for themselves as a couple brought great peace, togetherness and resolution.

Darrell and Anthea, on the other hand, had no marriage preparation and more or less fell headlong into marriage without too much of a thought as to the challenges they might face, and face them they did! As they say in the introduction to the Sozo for Couples manual:

"Ours is a marriage that has developed, matured and got better as the years have passed, which sounds great until you look at this another way, which is that if we'd only known then what we know now, life together would have been a great deal less painful."

It's to help all couples considering marriage to avoid the pitfalls they experienced that they, with Liz, created the Sozo for Couples' ministry, of which this book is a part.

Just to mention: Sozo for Couples isn't just for marrieds! We would encourage all couples to have regular individual Sozos as well as a Sozo for Couples as part of their marriage preparation, and then to have these regularly once they are married as a form of marriage check-up.

(If you're wondering what Sozo is and why we keep mentioning it a good place to start finding out would be the Bethel Sozo UK website, www.bethelsozo.org.uk.)

STARTING OUT

Introduction

Why would anyone need a marriage preparation book like this? Surely we just look into the limpid pools of each other's eyes, fall in love and before you know where you are you're married and living happily ever after? That may well be but unfortunately statistics tell us another and much sadder story: that more marriages in the western world are failing than succeeding. It appears that we're just as capable of falling out of love as in love, but whereas the experience of falling in love was soft and gooey, the falling out of love is traumatic, deeply hurtful and causes untold family heartache.

So, here's the challenge, how do we stop this frightening trend? How do we, or more to the point you, make your marriage successful? What does it even mean to be successfully married? We have had many long marriages in our respective families but neither of us would call all of these a 'success', even though, for many both in and outside the Church, the fact that the marriage lasted through to "death us do part" would be enough to qualify it as one.

Here's the deal, in John 10:10[NIV], Jesus says "...I have come that they may have life, and have it to the full", which would suggest that our lives should be full of life, vitality, fun and good things, and that applies to our marriages too.

How do we do that? How can we ensure that our marriage is long lasting and has life, or is it inevitable that as the years pass by our love and tolerance of each other slowly dwindles? And before you give this thought too much room, the answer is, firmly, 'No'. This book shows you how to lay a foundation that enables you to do just that. Research shows that engaging in marriage preparation not only reduces the risk of divorce but helps build healthy, vibrant, long lasting relationships, so well done for starting in this book!

As you read you'll find that we've given you various points to engage with. These will either be:

'Thought Stops!' – where you should both stop, answer the questions on your own and then discuss your answers with each other. These discussions between you will be really important. Take your time! You may even want to involve a third-party facilitator in these discussions to help you unpack the depths of some of the questions asked.

or

'Sozo Stops!' – at which point we want you to stop, ask God the questions, and listen to what He has to tell you.

Sometimes these 'Sozo Stops' will suggest a question for you to ask Father God on your own and then to discuss what He tells you with your partner. Sometimes there'll be something for both of you to ask together and then discuss. Either way the more time you spend talking stuff through, the more secure your relational foundations will be.

If you find yourself stuck on any of the Sozo Stops!, or challenged in a way that causes you to feel uneasy, have an individual Sozo! Contact us at answers@sozoforcouples.org and we'll send you an application form for a Sozo via Zoom.

Here's a 'Thought Stop!' to start you off:

Thought Stop

Why do you want to get married?

Favorite! Because 10 years already happy and don't want to marry anyone else.

What would you say is your partner's reason for marrying you?

Loves me. want to be forever.

At the 'Thought Stops!' try and get beyond the obvious. If you've both answered "Because I love you" to the first of the above, try again, drill down and really get to grips with exactly what it is that's brought you to this place of wanting to be married.

Ultimately there are many reasons why people decide to tie the knot. For some it may be that they feel absolutely in love with their partner and they want to spend the rest of their lives together. For others it's the need for stability and the hope that they'll find it in marriage. Others again get married because they don't want to be single and the person in front of them seems suitable. And then there's the sexual side of marriage and wanting to have that within a committed relationship. Many feel that the person they're with has been chosen by God for them to marry. The desire to have children may motivate others. Simply not wanting to be alone as the years pass can be a strong motivation too. It could also be about fulfilling the expectations of parents or grandparents or society. There are so many reasons and we haven't even touched on any legal, financial, cultural or religious reasons there may be!

None of these reasons are necessarily 'bad' but they may not be the best reasons – if your intention is to enjoy a long and successful marriage. So, let's go back to first principals and see what the Biblical reasons for getting married are.

Read through just the first few pages of the Bible and in Genesis 2:18^{NIV} you'll find, "The Lord God said, 'It is not good for the man to be alone. I will make a helper suitable for him.'"

God did not design us for a life spent alone. After all, He doesn't live alone Himself, He's Three in One – Father, Son and Spirit. God has always been about relationship and He always will be! Jesus died to reconcile our relationship with God and with each other. It's not surprising that He wants us to live in in a good connected relationship with each other in marriage.

In John 5:19^{NIV} Jesus is talking to His accusers when He says, "Very truly I tell you, the Son can do nothing by himself; He can do only what He sees his Father doing, because whatever the Father does the Son also does." Jesus only did what He saw His Father doing. How was He able to do that? Because He had connection and a relationship with His Father.

There is in all of us an innate desire for relationship and connection but sometimes we can be a like a broken jigsaw piece: we want to connect, we may even know where we fit and we may be able to see what the big picture looks like, but we have to get patched up and regain our shape to make the jigsaw whole. That's why it's so important that when we come to consider getting married we make the effort and spend time discovering our broken pieces. We then need to work on ourselves so that when the time comes we've regained our shape and can connect fully.

Marriage is about intimacy or, looked at another way, 'into me, you see'. For some of us the idea of allowing another person to look into us, or even for us to look into ourselves, is scary. Introspection will be painful if we've experienced past hurts or brokenness. Others will have picked up a broken image of intimacy and connect marriage with sex rather than relationship. We're all different and bring different thoughts, experiences and expectations to marriage, but one thing is for sure, intimacy is at the absolute heart of relationship and marriage is about the closest relationship you can have. So we're going to spend some time exploring what true intimacy can look like and set you off on the path of building this with your partner. It will be fun!

It's also possible, of course, that some of you reading this and working through the exercises with your partner are in for a bit of a shock. You may realise that you're not as compatible as you had both first thought and that getting married isn't such a good idea after all. As difficult as coming to this realisation may be, we'd strongly advise and encourage you to make the hard choice now, before going any further. It may seem impossible if you are in the middle of wedding planning to break off the relationship but it is better to do it now before children and property become an issue and have to be broken apart. We're sorry, but that's the truth!

Chapter One

Purpose

For a number of years Liz and Stuart organised a marriage seminar at a large Christian conference. They used to begin by asking those attending what they thought the purpose of marriage was. The answers back would vary: to be happy; to have children; to be together; to have sex; but very few people would actually think of the bigger picture and give the answer Liz and Stuart were hoping to hear, the purpose of our marriage is to fulfil whatever God's purpose for our marriage is..

Is this something either of you have ever thought about? It's one thing to have dreams, even plans, but what are these based on? Our suggestion and recommendation is that everything should be based on our purpose.

Where would be a good place to start on the subject of purpose? First of all, let's look at the purpose of marriage. We have already seen that God's intention is that we shouldn't be alone. But for each of us (as individuals, couples and families), God also has a destiny call, a purpose for our lives, so a good place to start is with this question:

What is the Kingdom purpose for our marriages? We are talking about all Christian marriages here, not just yours.

The easy answer is to quote Jeremiah 29:11[NIV:] "For I know the plans I have for you," declares the Lord, "plans to prosper you and not to harm you, plans to give you hope and a future."

This is great, but what does it mean? Maybe this could be better read as "I want you to have hope and a future and I'll give you plans that will lead to prosperity and wholeness." What this clearly says to us is that He, God, wants us to be happy and that we'll achieve happiness by following the plans that He'll give us. And that's the point, happiness and fulfilment doesn't come from following our plans and dreams but His plans and dreams for us. And that's what we call purpose, because once you know what His plans for you are, individually and as a couple, you'll know your purpose.

Purpose, then, is linked with our identity as a person. It's the big question about who God has made you to be. In a marriage the purpose will be linked to the two identities coming together and making a new one. Genesis 2:24[NIV] expresses this well: "That is why a man leaves his father and mother and is united to his wife, and they become one flesh." In other words, they carry a new and unique Godly purpose, which could be being pioneers, hope bringers, lovers of the unlovable etc. Our purpose really paints that big picture of what God has for our marriage. If either or both of you have never spent time thinking about your own individual purpose then now would be a good time to do so, because your individual purposes really need to inform your purpose as a married couple. They don't have to be the same, although that would be good, but they do need to be able to co-exist or, even better, be complementary to each other.

Those of us who are beyond the first flush of our marriages will agree that love needs a rationale to exist, in other words, a deeper reason for being married than just the obvious physical attraction. Even the enjoyment of shared experience requires something deeper. When you think about it, that deeper something is our shared hopes and expectations for the future, in other words, a shared vision. Our suggestion is that, in a godly marriage, vision should have as its root a shared purpose, a knowledge of what God has destined you both for. So, for example, if our shared purpose is to love the unlovable, then our shared vision might be to work with excluded groups in society. One precedes the other. Your vision should support your purpose.

A marriage needs a clear and shared purpose leading to the vision a couple will develop between them and share as something for them to work towards. If I don't know what my spouse's purpose is, how can we share vision and how can I meet their deep needs and the desires of their heart? If I don't know what my spouse's purpose is, I'll probably continually disappoint and even alienate her/him. And, of course, if she/he doesn't know what really drives me, what my purpose and vision are, then my needs won't be met either. We will then both be skating around each other on a superficial level, trying to make each other happy whilst not being happy ourselves.

Shared purpose and vision are the bedrock of a happy marriage. And our values, the way we do life, stem from that vision. If our vision is to be passionate about God, then our values will ensure we live our lives accordingly. Our vision might include how we raise our children or what we do with our work lives, but so long as our vision, our purpose and our values are shared, then we'll be a long way towards knowing what each other's expectations are and they won't be mismatched. This whole idea of a good marriage being one in which a couple has a shared purpose is vitally important, not just for our spouses but for ourselves. Stephen De Silva has done some excellent work on what he calls 'The Purpose Train' in his Prosperous Soul teaching and we use this concept, with thanks for his permission.

Thought Stop!

What would you say is God's purpose for your marriage?

What steps do you need to take in your relationship to live in this purpose?

What do you hope to achieve through your marriage?

What is your purpose in life, and do you share this with your partner?

How will you attain your purpose?

_____

_____

_____

_____

Often, we get our purpose and vision muddled! For example, how would it be if you thought that your purpose in marriage was to have children? No doubt this will work for you during your child bearing years and having a family, but what happens if you can't have children or when the childbearing years are past? Can you see how what you thought was your purpose was really no more than one part of a much larger picture, a small part of the vision?

Our purpose, then, is the really big picture stuff – why you were created? Why did God make you? What has God made you for?

To help you understand this better, here is Liz and Stuart's purpose...

Their Purpose as a couple (the big picture): To be pioneers.

Their Vision (what that looks like): Parenting/raising up revivalists and Kingdom reformers.

Their Strategy: (how they achieve their Vision): By teaching, modelling, training, equipping, empowering and releasing.

Their Tactics (the day to day working out of their strategy): Family, partnerships, conferences, relationships, running a School of Supernatural Ministry, running a Church, being involved in Sozo ministry.

And here is Anthea and Darrell's purpose...-

Their Purpose (the big picture): To create open spaces that allow people to know who they are and what they can achieve so that they walk in the fullness of God's destiny plan for them.

Their Vision (what that looks like): To equip the equippers, whoever and wherever they are.

Their Strategy (how they achieve their Vision): By teaching, mentoring, networking, encouraging and loving.

Their Tactics (the day to day working out of their strategy): Writing, intercession, prophetic ministry, Sozo, Sozo for Couples, leading a Life Group, Sozo teams.

Knowing one's purpose as a couple is a huge help in keeping a marriage on track. It helps give clarity when making choices and what to spend time, money and energy on. Knowing one's purpose and the purpose for your marriage will give you joint goals for you to work towards together.

If, as you both think about your purpose, you find you have entirely different views on life and that your individual purposes are completely incompatible with each other, what do you do then? It may be time to ask those tough questions about the purpose of your relationship. It may be time to ask God if you have any ideas about your purpose that He may not want you to have. Then again, it may be that you have no idea what your purpose is as a couple. Don't worry, you can ask God – you don't have to figure this out on your own.

The first 'Sozo Stop!' will help you with that. If, after this, you are still not sure then some couples find it helpful to chat it through with a mature Christian or your pastor. We also suggest that having an individual Sozo session at this point will help you prepare for marriage- if you want more information on this check out the website information at the back of the book.

Sozo Stop!

Father God what do you see as the purpose for our marriage?

_____

_____

_____

Father God are there any barriers to us stepping into that purpose?

_____

_____

_____

_____

Father God how do you want to deal with those barriers?

Things that can get in the way

Chapter Two

Expectations

Still with us? We hope so!

Now you've spent some time working together to identify what your purpose in life is, let's turn to what our expectations of each other in marriage may be. When you think about it, all we can ever really bring to a new marriage is our experience of marriages we've known. Of course, we bring an element of learned knowledge too, but experience typically forms the basis of our pre-conceptions. Now if you've been married before what follows might not apply to you in the same way, but it will to a degree.

The thing is, if your only real experience of marriage is your parents, then your experience of their relationship will inevitably largely colour your idea of what marriage will be like going forward. If your parents have or had a loving close relationship, that's what you'll be expecting. If they were continually fighting you may not be heading into your marriage consciously expecting that, because you love each other and the last thing you want is a marriage like your parents, but somewhere deep inside there'll be a bit of you that knows what can happen and much as you'll fight against it part of you is just waiting for the worst to happen. To a degree and unless you're aware of it and have openly discussed this potential pitfall with your partner, it's almost as if your parents are marrying theirs, the product of one set of expectations marrying another. To which we all loudly say, "Heaven forbid!"

It's these expectations and, sometimes, unmet expectations, which can really make relationships fail. Of course, you could argue that we're all fallen and that therefore failure is the natural state of affairs in our (unredeemed) state. But you could equally argue that, on the other hand, as Christians we're new creations, if we stay close to God we should stay close to each other and therefore not succumb to relational failure. The truth is tough that many Christian marriages do fail, so why is that? And one immediate answer is that our expectations are often based on lies. But before we look at this:

▨▨▨ Thought Stop!

Having read the above, what expectations have you from, and for your marriage?

How does that match the relationship you witnessed in your parents' marriage?

What would you like your relationship to look like in 10 years' time?

What do you think your partner's expectations are for how your relationship will look in 10 years' time?

What do you think could get in the way?

Hopefully you took some time to think about your answers before you discussed these with your partner. Hopefully, also, you now have a clearer idea of how one's experience can cloud one's expectations. The aim here is for you both to be able to get off on the right foot with neither of you believing lies about what could happen in the future or having false expectations of each other. That's not to say that you'll definitely share a lifetime of wedded bliss together but it is to say that if you don't expect any blips along the way and your marriage falls to pieces the moment your relationship comes under pressure then maybe you haven't entered this relationship with your eyes as wide open as you should.

Just to be sure, ask Father God these questions:

Sozo Stop!

Father God, am I believing any lies about marriage?

(If so) Father God, who do I need to forgive for my believing those lies?

22

Forgive them, whoever it is, and then ask:

Father God, what's the truth about marriage that you want me to carry forward and base my belief and behaviour on?

Things that can get in the way

Chapter Three

Around Communications

If false expectations can cause problems, how about miscommunications?

The Bible's point about the tongue revealing the heart is so true (Matthew 15:18) but there's a lot more to it. When we speak, our words express meaning but they also communicate emotion. Therefore, miscommunication can be as much about the way words are said or received as their actual content. Luke 6:31 tells us to do to others as we would have them do to us, but that's not the complete story. We should really treat and speak to our partners as they want to be treated and spoken to, which might be quite a different thing altogether. This will be especially true if our partners have words of affirmation as their love language or have any history of verbal abuse in their past.

Many of us think that because we can articulate our thoughts well then we must be masters of communication. Few things can be further from the truth. In fact being articulate can create a barrier rather than overcome it, particularly when language is being used unkindly, to browbeat, shut down or overwhelm one's partner. No one likes being treated like a child and spoken down to. In fact most of us are even slightly uncomfortable when people do the opposite and treat us as someone special and put us on a pedestal.

We're most happy when we're treated as responsible adults and talked to as equals, creating an atmosphere conducive to mutual acceptance and relationship. Your partner will have an expectation of what good communication and loving expression sounds and feels like. Being able to use and express the right words to honour your partner will work wonders in a relationship. It's also worth mentioning here that it has been suggested that on average and given free rein, women will speak an average of 20,000 words per day whilst men scarcely manage 7,000. Make of that what you will!

Belonging to, or identifying with, different socio-economic classes can also affect our communication. A study done by Hart and Risley at the University of Kansas found that children in a professional family were exposed to 215,000 words a week whilst in a working-class family this dropped to 125,000. In a family on welfare the figure became 62,000 words a week. If you and your partner come from different socio-economic backgrounds, it's worth reflecting how this can influence the way the two of you communicate with each other. Some of us are used to saying a lot with an extensive vocabulary but for others this can feel totally overwhelming.

Miscommunication is very often found not so much in what you're saying but in how you're listening. When people feel that they're not being listened to it challenges their every shred of self-esteem and self-confidence and, again, this will be especially true if their love language is quality time. So often we're not really listening to what's being said because we're busy thinking of the reply we're going to make. Someone for whom being listened to is important will pick this up immediately and they'll be looking out for it. Giving people one's full attention when they're talking to us is so important.

Understanding the pace of each other's communication is helpful too. This can be affected by whether we are an external processor, speaking out whatever comes into our head or whether we like to ponder internally before speaking. Learning to give each other the space to respond to communication in the ways you both need can deepen your relationship.

Thought Stop!

What kind of language did you hear growing up? Was it kind or unkind, pure or full of bad words, attacking and argumentative, controlling, cynical, accusing, conciliatory, peaceful, loving…?

Did both your parents use the same sort of language? Should they have?

How did living with that language make you feel?

What language would you like to see in your marriage? Is that what you're experiencing in your relationship now?

▓▓▓▓ Sozo Stop!

Father God, how would you like me to speak to my husband /wife to be? How do I learn?

Things that can get in the way

Chapter Four

Around Attention

Do you feel loved and affirmed in your relationship? Do you get to spend as much time together as you want? Are you OK spending time on your own, doing your own thing? Do you even look forward to having 'you' time away from your partner?

It's one thing to enjoy each other's company and want to share and be close at all times, but it's quite another to need this to be the case. Placing unreasonable expectations on your partner and your relationship will cause problems, and unreasonable here means in the eye and opinion of your partner. If they're expecting to be able to go out for evenings with the boys/girls and you want them to stay in with you, then there is a problem. If they want to do something that makes you feel threatened and unloved then your expectations and theirs are dangerously different and you need to work on resolving this together before you go much further.

Expectations around the amount and degree of attention required by either of you can cause huge relational issues, especially if one of you has a level of self-esteem that needs constant affirmation, and that's before you have a row! People talk about men retreating to their 'man-cave' if they become offended or hurt, hiding in there and pretending that all's well whilst speaking in monosyllables. It's a mistake, though, to think that women don't also retreat into a cave, but theirs tends to be of a different nature. Women can also become passive-aggressive, sometimes quite publicly, but ultimately both behaviours result from unmet expectations, hurts and unmet needs. You both need to know how to apologise, deal with it and rise above this behaviour.

Thought Stop!

Would you consider yourself to be a generally needy person? If not, are you 'high maintenance'? Under what conditions or circumstances do you become needy?

How about your partner, are they generally needy or 'high maintenance'? Are they needy in certain circumstances? If so, how do you handle this?

How do you typically react when you're hurt or offended? Do you withdraw, get angry or passive aggressive...or something else?

When you react in this way, what gets you out of it?

What do you think about the idea of being totally dependent on each other, wanting or needing to be with each other all the time? How good or bad is it in a marriage?

How does your partner typically react when they are hurt or offended? Do they withdraw, get angry, passive aggressive or something else?

When your partner reacts in this way what gets them out of it?

Sozo Stop!

Father God, where did my expectations in this area come from?

Father God, what would you say to me about these expectations?

Father God, what do I need to change in me to re-set my expectations to what they should be?

Things that can get in the way

Chapter Five

Around Finances

Love of money is said to be the root of all kinds of evil. We'd suggest that fear is a more likely contender for that dubious honour, however money is definitely at the root of falling out in relationships. If there's one thing that's guaranteed to get between you and married bliss, it's money, in fact money is generally considered to be the second most likely reason for divorce after infidelity.

When we enter a relationship we often come with very different expectations and priorities concerning money. Arguments about money will often revolve around whose money it is anyway and what and how much should be spent. Dig below the surface and you'll often find that such arguments are caused by a perceived (or actual) lack of sufficient income or unmet expectations around each other's willingness or ability to earn. The root causes of such arguments are inevitably embedded in the unaddressed experiences of our past and the lies that have taken hold because of these. The way that one's parents handled and responded to money, or the lack of it, will invariably have a big influence on our own views of money.

It will often be the case that those who are overcautious about spending can have a 'fear door' open that makes them afraid to take risks with their money. Some people have a saving mentality, others are spenders. For others money issues may highlight a poverty mindset or an orphan spirit. For those with a poverty mindset (a way of thinking and being that bases every purchase on cheapness, need and a fear of lack) it is impossible to dream big in the area of finances and this can, for example, squash the aspirations of a partner who might see an opportunity and want to invest in it.

Can you see how important it is to discuss money issues at this point in your relationship and to understand your partner's approach to thoughts and beliefs around the whole subject. You really need to be on the same page in your approach to earning and spending to ensure harmony in your relationship.

Thought Stop!

How would you describe your approach to money? What was your experience growing up?

What would you do if you had a million? How much of it would you save or invest or give away?

What would lack of money look like to you? How easy or difficult would it be for you to cope with? What would just enough money look like to you?

How do you think your partner would describe their approach to money? What do you know about their experience of money growing up?

What do you think your partner would do if they had £1m/$1m? How much of it would they save or invest or give away?

How do you think your partner would cope with having little money? How easy or difficult would it be for them? What would not enough look like to them?

Sozo Stop!

Father God, am I believing any lies about money and provision? What's your truth?

Father God, how do I re-set my thinking about money and provision to reflect the truth you've shown me?

STARTING OUT

Things that can get in the way

Chapter Six

Around Boundaries

You may think that we dealt with this when considering Expectations Around Attention in Chapter Four, but there's a difference between having a partner who needs your attention to feed their self-confidence and one who just has a different opinion to you as to what commitment looks like and involves. Both these behaviours share the same outworking, the 'where are you going and why?' type of situation. Whilst the need for attention has a deep root that can often be addressed by a good Sozo, issues around boundaries may be much easier to deal with and just need a dose of understanding, good will and mutual agreement. Having said this, don't assume this to be the case. Boundary issues can also have deep roots, often going back to childhood family issues.

Let's take a fairly common scenario. She expects him to come home from work, have dinner and share the rest of what's left of the day with her. He wants/needs to get to the gym after work for a couple of hours to keep fit and work out the stresses of the day. You see, neither of this couple are necessarily right or wrong but then neither of their expectations will be met if they both insist on getting their way. If both of them stick their heels in and demand that their expectations are met, this relationship will deteriorate rather quickly. Instead they need to discuss together the best way that their needs can be met.

The truth is that mutually accepted boundaries are vital for all couples. Both parties have to understand what's you, what's me and what's us and then work within the boundaries of each of them, and of the world they live in.

Whilst on the subject of boundaries it's also important to take on board that these do not only apply to time. They can equally apply to emotions, friendships, parents, Church involvement and other areas of life where expectations can be threatened by one of the couple investing in an activity or relationship perceived as detrimental of the other.

▰▰▰ Thought Stop!

How much of your life at the moment is just you, and how important is it to you?

Would you give any of it up for the sake of your relationship? How would that feel?

How prepared are you to share in your partner's wider life and interests?

How prepared are you to allow your partner to share your wider life interests?

What would being excluded, voluntarily or otherwise from your partner's wider life and interests, feel like?

Are you someone who feels you should share all your interests with your partner, or just some? How importance is this to you?

Sozo Stop!

Father God, am I being over-protective of my boundaries in any way? What's the lie I'm believing in this?

Father God, how do I re-set my boundaries so they work to benefit my relationship with my partner?

Things that can get in the way

Chapter Seven

Around Habits

The heading 'Habits' isn't really meant to be a euphemism, but it is a bit of a cover all. Habits can cover everything from the way you stir your tea through to the worst behavioural excesses. Here, we want you to consider 'habits' as being anything that may act as an impediment in your relationship.

We have a habit(!) in the first flush of relationship to gloss over negative or unhelpful behaviours and traits we see in our partners. We even find them charming and make excuses for them, which works for a time, until, that is, that behaviour starts to irritate or upset. Until, that is, it becomes an issue between you. The problem then is that it's a problem and the problem with problems is that the bigger the problem the harder it is to talk about. Which is why we suggest you talk about habits now.

In case you're not sure what to include here are a few:

Swearing, blasphemy, drinking, over-drinking, drunkenness, drug taking of any kind, over medication, smoking, coffee, tea, biting your fingernails, watching certain programmes on TV, fast food, emotional shopping, spending on credit cards, Facebook or other social media, sweets, sugar, comfort eating, mobile phone addiction, video games, unpleasant personal habits, hygiene problems, over working, over exercising, pornography, lying, stealing, negative self-talk, procrastinating, people pleasing, breaking promises to yourself, checking the mirror, spending a lot of time online, gambling, physical abuse, verbal abuse, self-pity, temper, critical spirit, being over argumentative, driving too fast, leaving the toilet seat up, leaving the top off the toothpaste, leaving clothes lying around, not shutting the door…

The list is endless and this one is anything but exhaustive but go through it and use it to bring others to mind. Note also that not all these are equal. There's a difference between recognising and being willing to address ungodly behaviours and being willing to change a habit.

▨▨▨ Thought Stop!

What habits of yours could be annoying to your partner?

Would you be willing to put effort into changing your habit to please your partner? Which would be the easiest one to start with?

What habits of theirs could or do annoy you?

What would happen if they escalated?

What do you think would be the best way to discuss this with your partner without it upsetting them?

What would be the best way for your partner to discuss this with you, without it upsetting you?

███████ Sozo Stop!

Father God, what would you say about those of my habits my partner doesn't like?

42

Father God, do I carry any resentment about this? If so, what lies am I believing? What's the truth? How do I adopt this truth into my life?

Things that can get in the way:

Chapter Eight

Around Sex

Such an interesting topic when it comes to marriage preparation! It's a bit like the elephant in the room in that it's not something one would necessarily discuss over dinner but, to a point, it should be. What we mean is that sex needs to be talked about openly in your relationship even before you get married. Like all the other topics we've covered under the 'Things that can get in the way' heading, sex is something that unless it's clearly understood between you could cause untold stress and relational damage. Let's be clear. Sex has to be mutually desired rather than demanded. Forced sex, even in marriage is still rape. The truth is that continual self-sacrifice by having sex with your partner when you don't want to will invariably lead to problems down the line.

You probably don't need to be told this but it's not unusual for males and females to have different expectations of each other when it comes to sex. It may be truer to say that men and women are made differently and that their desires in this area may differ. Perhaps oddly, what sometimes can happen is that we can get into a pattern of assuming that we both know each other's wants and needs but never, for whatever reason, communicate these to each other. This can easily result in mismatched expectations. Good communication is vital to a good sex life. The more the two of you are able to discuss your needs and desires openly with each other in a loving way, the better your sex life and relationship will be. Maintaining an emotional closeness to your partner often increases the desire for physical intimacy, especially in women. Another thing: sex is such an important issue that it, or the withholding of it, should never be used as a bargaining tool or to control, manipulate or punish the other person.

Whatever your past, the more open you can be with each other the better! In this relationship you're on a voyage of discovery with each other. It's so important to remember this, especially in your early days together and especially if one or other of you have little or no past experience of making love. There's a great phrase which talks about going from Zero to Hero overnight, and if you think you have to be like this, don't. Take nothing for granted, expect to make mistakes, expect things not to work out all the time, laugh about them, share the moment and enjoy one of God's great gifts.

Thought Stop!

Is there anything about your past your partner doesn't know? If so, would it be better to tell them now, rather than for them to find out about it later? Do you fear how they would respond or that they may no longer respect you or want to be with you?

How would you feel if you were to discover at a later date that your partner had kept something important from you, something you would have wanted to know about?

Do you have any experiences, fears or reservations about sex that you've kept bottled up? Does sex feel like an embarrassing or dirty thing, or something that shouldn't be talked about?

What would stop you being open about these, if they exist, or anything else to do with sex with your partner?

Sozo Stop!

Father God, are there any lies I'm believing about sex? Who do I need to forgive for these?

After you've prayed forgiveness,
Father God, what is the truth about sex that you want me to know and live from?

In Conclusion:

Let's be clear, there's no shame in having mismatched expectations – not until the blame game kicks in, and the blame game will only kick in if you allow it. You could say that expectations only become mismatched when we don't agree with them, and that any unmet expectations are down to us, not our partner. But that's assuming that all our partner's expectations are acceptable and generally reasonable, and they may not be, depending on what he or she experienced growing up. Now really is the best time for you to be discussing these so you know exactly what you expect from each other, what's acceptable and what isn't.

Needs however, are different. All of us need love, we need to be affirmed, we need security and significance! If we didn't receive these from our parents or from someone else as we were growing up we're going to bring these needs into our marriage in the shape of unhealthy or unrealistic expectations for our partner to meet. However, the reality is that it isn't our partner's job to meet these needs and, besides, they will be bringing their own expectations to the party. That's what we're dealing with. What happens then is that couples may get stuck in unhealthy ways of responding or, more to the point, unhealthy conflict. They start to engage in war rather than diplomacy or they hide and sweep things under the carpet rather than deal with them. Men retreat to the caves we mentioned earlier, potentially opening the door for a passive-aggressive cycle to kick in. As a result, conversation soon becomes a competition of 'I win-you lose' instead of 'we both win'. All this can be avoided if it's dealt with before it starts, and the way to do this is by really getting to know each other, which is why going through this book should help you!

Sozo Stop!

Father God, have I placed unfair expectations on my partner? Where did I learn these?

_____

_____

_____

Father God, who do I need to forgive for teaching me these expectations?

_____

_____

_____

Father God, I choose to forgive _____ for _____

Father God, what has been the effect on my life of these expectations?

Father God, what lie have I believed?

Father God, I renounce the lie

Father God, what truth do you want me to know?

48

Father God, how will this truth affect our relationship?

Chapter Nine

What's Expected of You in your Marriage?

In previous chapters we've talked about expectations in relationships, namely the sorts of expectations that we have and carry as a result of our own upbringing and background. There's a whole different set of expectations out there as well, these ones being the expectations that society and the culture we live in place on us. These impact and affect every area of life, not least marriage, so let's look at some.

A good place to start is with what most people would consider as being the 'traditional' role-based model of marriage. This is the one where we think the man is dominant and the women submissive and each of the couple's roles are clearly defined. He's the provider, she the homemaker. He's the decision maker and she just has to agree with those decisions. You might recognise this model as being one you've witnessed with the older generation and promised yourself that you'll never agree to a relationship that looks anything like this. However, there are good things about this model, not least that the roles are clear and defined. The challenge is that dominant can easily become domineering and that such a marriage can stop both members of the couple from being able to grow in the relationship. We probably all have relatives who have had this sort of relationship. Did you ever think that they could have achieved so much more if they had been free to grow and express themselves? Sometimes the Church has pushed this traditional marriage model as being Biblical and here's the good news: it's absolutely not!

Then we have what we'll call the 'modern' contract model of marriage, where both of the couple are seen as equal in role and identity. With this model personal rights are important. If one person has a night out, the other person puts this in the bank and has a night out too, to make up for it. If one spends £50/ $50 then the other can spend £50/$50 as well. It's a model that can so easily become a tussle between two people about what they perceive as their 'rights' in the marriage. Pushed to a logical conclusion you get to the situation where everything has to be divided equally – workload, who provides, who takes care of the children/home, everything! It can sound like a good way to do marriage but it can also lead to confusion as both parties are keeping a score and the scores may not tally!, with no clear roles defined and an embedded sense of entitlement – you did this so I should be allowed to do this too. Do you know a couple like that? Who do you know whose relationship looks like a tug of war?

We've had the 'traditional' and 'modern' contract, but how about the 'Biblical'? What's the Biblical viewpoint on marriage?

Let's look at Ephesians 5:21-31^{NIV}:

21   *Submit to one another out of reverence for Christ.*

22   *Wives, submit yourselves to your own husbands as you do to the Lord.*

23   *For the husband is the head of the wife as Christ is the head of the church, his body, of which he is the Saviour.*

24   *Now as the church submits to Christ, so also wives should submit to their husbands in everything.*

25   *Husbands, love your wives, just as Christ loved the church and gave himself up for her*

26   *to make her holy, cleansing her by the washing with water through the word,*

27   *and to present her to himself as a radiant church, without stain or wrinkle or any other blemish, but holy and blameless.*

28   *In this same way, husbands ought to love their wives as their own bodies. He who loves his wife loves himself.*

29   *After all, no one ever hated their own body, but they feed and care for their body, just as Christ does the church—*

30   *for we are members of his body.*

31   *For this reason a man will leave his father and mother and be united to his wife, and the two will become one flesh."*

Note that we've started at verse 21, not verse 22 as often happens...

Verse 21 says "Submit to one another" but did you know that this is the only time the word 'submit' is used in the whole passage? The translators, for ease of reading and to enhance the meaning, repeated it in verse 22, even though it isn't in the original text. The idea is that at the beginning of the passage, where Paul is talking, he's referring not just to husbands and wives, but to masters and slaves, parents and children and what he's saying to all these people is that we should submit to each other!

How do you think that went down at the time? It was revolutionary! Imagine if everyone who heard that message was to approach their relationships with an attitude of submission! And remember, submission does not mean subservience, but it does mean having a healthy heart attitude towards one another.

Then we have Verse 22, where we see wives are to submit to their husbands as to the Lord. Remember, in the original Greek text it doesn't mention 'submit' again here because it's already been said in Verse 21. It's a reminder that this is something wives need to do but is not reserved just for women, it's for husbands as well!

The message is in the last few words. How does Jesus treat the Church? He treats her with a sacrificial love that brings intimacy, a submission that draws us closer. This is the model Jesus wants us to follow in our marriages, something made clear in verse 25 when He says to husbands that they should love their wives just as Christ loved the Church and gave Himself up for her.

Wow! What a different way to look at life – a lifestyle in which a husband sacrificially gives of himself for the good of his wife, as Jesus did for the Church. A husband willing to give his life for hers, to literally die for her if necessary. This then becomes a relationship where, in response, submission from the wife towards the husband brings connection, intimacy and closeness, both physically and emotionally, and vice versa.

Unfortunately, so many husbands have misunderstood their role and thought that it gives them dominance, that being the 'head' is about control and authority when actually it's about sacrifice and service. Ultimately what a husband is absolutely responsible for is the creation of a family atmosphere where all can thrive and grow in their submission to Christ. In fact, the more he sacrificially gives, the more he will see his bride able to submit willingly.

Marriage with this understanding is not about a jostling for power or about who gets to be the boss but about intimacy, love, sacrifice, mutual submission and everyone fulfilling their identity and destiny in Christ. The Biblical view of marriage is therefore about a 'covenant' model, with both people committed to serving each other.

We hope you're OK with that, because next we're now going to look at what makes a good Biblical marriage.

Thought Stop!

What do you feel or think or believe is the role of a man in a marriage? If the husband-to-be: Would you then be satisfied and happy filling this role in your marriage? If the wife-to-be: Would you be happy for your future husband to fulfil this role?

What do you feel is the role of a woman in a marriage? If the husband-to-be: Do you feel, think or believe that your partner is ready, willing and able to fulfil this role? If the wife-to-be: Would you be satisfied and happy filling this role in your marriage?

Sozo Stop!

Father God, is there any one I need to forgive for teaching me a wrong view of marriage?

Father God, could you show me how you want me to be in our relationship and in our marriage?

Chapter Ten

A Biblical Marriage

What doesn't make a good marriage is one in which in which the husband gets to Proverbs 27:15 [TPT], (parenthesis added) and, nodding wisely, reads:

> *An endless drip, drip, drip, from a leaky tap [faucet] and the words of a cranky, nagging wife have the same effect.*

Actually, we don't think that nagging is purely a wifely activity and we're not saying this because we think we have to. Men are more than capable of nagging, although it may not present itself in quite the same way. The point here is that, whoever is doing the nagging, it's usually as a result of unhappiness and not being heard plus a bad habit not being changed. If a couple have clear, understood and reciprocated lines of communication and a heartfelt desire to please the other, nagging won't happen. Promise. But what's vital is the whole communications thing.

Intimacy and communication

It's no surprise that communication and the intimacy that invariably stems from it are foundational for a good Biblical marriage. Before Liz married Stuart they spent a lot of time talking with each other. They would talk about anything and everything – from everyday life to the big issues of their hearts, to dreams and their hopes for the future. They still do, because over nearly 30 years of marriage they've changed, and they constantly need to update each other and themselves. What Liz wanted when she was 22 is very different to her hopes now and Stuart needs to know this, as much as she needs to know how Stuart's thinking has also changed. It's having had a good friendship as a basis of their marriage that has helped them to weather the storms they have gone through.

Darrell and Anthea, on the other hand, hardly knew each other when they got married. Even though they had lived together for a few years, they had never spent much time talking the deep stuff and really had no idea what each other's dreams and aspirations were, if indeed they had any. As a result, they lived very much on the edge, burying issues and not talking about them – which is the way they had both learned to cope growing up in a dysfunctional family without brothers or sisters. There were a lot of rows. If only they had heard of John Gottman!

Gottman is an American psychological researcher and clinician who, over 40 years of research into marriage, came up with seven principles that he considered integral to a healthy marriage. What is really interesting, but shouldn't come as a surprise to us, is that his seven principles are all about communication and intimacy! Gottman talks about nurturing each other, being attentive and allowing oneself to be influenced by one's spouse, all stuff that is close to the heart of God. After all, He made us to be connected. He's a relational God, so it is no surprise that He wants us to have closeness and connection with each other. Gottman's principles are about really getting to know each other, learning to value each other, learning to turn to each other in challenges and paying attention to what your partner says – even if it is just a rambling thought. He also talks about learning how to value each other by the way you bring up issues softly and not harshly and learning to build a shared culture together.

Gottman's research was ground-breaking and remains one of the go-to places for marriage counsellors but, as mentioned above, nothing he talks about should come as a surprise to those of us who understand God's character. A Biblical marriage, then, is one in which we listen to our spouse's opinion rather than push our own. Where we as are interested in the details of our partner's thoughts and feelings as we are in their dreams and aspirations. Where we forgive quickly and don't hold onto offence and in which we really understand and value each other.

That's just on the communication side of your relationship. Proverbs has something to say about intimacy as well:

> *My son share your love with your wife alone. Drink from her well of pleasure and from no other.* Proverbs 5:15[TPT]

You can't get much clearer than that! Marriage is about one man and one woman committing to each other and forsaking all others. This means putting your relationship and connection with each other above all other relationships. That doesn't just mean other buddies or work mates, it means ALL relationships even with our computers and hobbies. They all have to come second to our relationship with each other and if you happen to be involved in Church life, yes, even our faith life and ministries have to come second! Only God and our relationship with Him should have a higher priority than out marriage.

It's this exclusivity in marriage that gives each of you the security to be yourselves and allows each of you to grow and flourish knowing you're safe. This faithfulness to each other is not claustrophobia but provides the secure foundation for both of you to grow and fulfil your destiny.

Here's another helpful quote from Proverbs, this time 5:18[TPT]

> *Your sex life will be blessed as you take joy and pleasure in the wife of your youth.*

And that's the truth, in a world where there is so much brokenness and where sex has become so many things it shouldn't be, a true Biblical marriage can be the safe place for sex to be brought back to what God intended it to be.

And God? Where does He come In?

A Biblical marriage has God right at its centre. Ecclesiastes 4:12[NLT] tells us that:

> *A person standing alone can be attacked and defeated, but two can stand back-to-back and conquer. Three are even better, for a triple-braided cord is not easily broken.*

And Ecclesiastes is absolutely right! A marriage where both partners are living their life in submission to God is a Biblical marriage. If both partners' wills are submitted to God's, then even in the tough moments they can come together and seek Him. It pulls you together when everything else seems like it's pushing you apart.

Thought Stop!

How have you thought about what a Biblical marriage looks like before now? How does this challenge your view?

What has been the 'type' of marriages you have seen in those close to you? E.g. traditional 'role-based', modern 'contract', Biblical 'covenant'.

How does this Biblical view of marriage challenge the current world view of marriage?

Sozo Stop!

Father God, is there anything in me that would hold me back from the level of intimacy I've just been reading about?

(If so) Father God, how do I deal with those things?

Chapter Eleven

Living with the Past

The inescapable truth is that we all have a past. It's what is in that past and how you deal with it that can really have an impact on your relationship now and in the future together.

You may be as innocent as the driven snow, but there's at least a chance that there is something there that you're not entirely proud of. So now's the time to be open and honest about it. Why? Because if you start off by being completely truthful with each other and place all your cards on the table it can bring a new and deeper closeness between you. In addition, and this is important, you don't want be going forward in your relationship with any shadows hanging over you.

Opening up about the truth of what's happened to you in the past might well be painful, but it will be considerably less painful now than in the future, the fact being that anything you hide, for whatever reason, will inevitably come back to bite you. It always does. This is going to be true for both of you but it's perhaps more so if the male partner holds things back. If you're the happy husband-to-be reading this, a word to the wise, never underestimate the degree to which your partner will need deep emotional connection and security to be able to fully express herself sexually.

So how do you deal with this past, other than being honest about it? The answer depends on how you feel about it and, more to the point, how your partner feels about it. If your attitude is one that says that the past is the past, let's move on, you may need to stop and think about that. If you're so gung-ho about the soul ties you've created in the past, what's going to be so different in the future. What could happen when the physical attraction and feelings you have right now become buried in the challenges of married life and all it means?

Soul Ties

We've just mentioned soul ties and you may not be aware of what these are. Here's an explanation. Sex involves body, soul and spirit, it's a tri-dimensional activity. Any time you have sex with someone you inevitably bond with them, it's part of having sex. It's worth considering what Dr Daniel Amen writes in his book, 'Change Your Brain, Change Your Life'. What he says is:

"Whenever a person is sexually involved with another person neurochemical changes occur in both their brains that encourage limbic, emotional, bonding. Limbic bonding is the reason that casual sex doesn't really work for most people on a whole mind and body level. Two people may decide to have sex 'just for the fun of it' yet something is occurring on another level that they may not have decided on at all: sex is enhancing an emotional bond between them whether they like it or not. One person, often the woman, is bound to form an attachment and will hurt when a casual affair ends. One reason it is usually the woman who is hurt the most is that the female limbic system is larger than the male's."

It's this bonding that creates what we call soul ties. Sex is like gluing two pieces of wood together and the next day ripping them apart. Of course, wood from the opposite board remains on each board. A piece of your sex partner (good, bad or ugly) stays with you, and vice versa, for the rest of your life, like it or not. Now imagine the impact if you were to have 'bonded' with multiple partners. Precisely!

Like it or not, unhealthy soul ties are often the residue from having had past partners with whom these life-long bonds have been created. You may only have had a short-term relationship with someone but it has long-term effects and these are what we're calling you to deal with now as you look forward to getting married. We would suggest that all soul ties need to be dealt with. None will be healthy, but some could be more unhealthy than others and these are the ones that you'll usually be much more aware of.

▨▨▨ Thought Stop!

Is there a past relationship, consummated or not that plays on your mind?

Do you think of someone from a past relationship or what happened during that relationship at any time?

When making an important decision, is there someone you need to mentally check in with to see if they would approve?

When you're with your partner do your thoughts ever slip to someone else? Have you ever called them by an ex-partner's name by mistake, or nearly done so?

Is there anyone from your past that you would insist on maintaining a relationship with, even though your partner didn't want you to?

Sozo Stop!

If you feel that there's someone with whom you have a soul tie then say this prayer:

> *"Father God, today I choose to break off any existing soul ties with x. I send back to them all ungodly memories, feeling, emotions or influences that I hold and I claim back from them today my purity / peace of mind / self respect / self worth / identity / voice / right to make decisions and anything else of mine that they have been holding and I wash these in the blood of Jesus and restore them to myself. In doing so I declare myself free of any soul tie that may have existed between us."*

And then we suggest you just ask Jesus this simple question: "Jesus is there anything more I need to do to break off this soul tie?" and listen and do what He says.

You may need to deal with as many soul ties as Father God shows you.

What we haven't mentioned yet is that one can have soul ties with things other than past boy/girl friends. We would suggest it's quite possible to have a soul tie with computer porn or an ungodly addiction of any other sort. If there's a lingering something there, it could even be one's parents, then there's a good chance there's a soul tie too. We would suggest you deal with these in much the same way as with soul ties with people.

Working Through Pain

Some of the memories you have around this whole area of past relationships could well be very painful. You may still be harbouring unforgiveness towards whoever is responsible for this pain and there could be a heap of shame attached as well. Let's look at and deal with unforgiveness and shame, because they're often at the root of this type pain...and who'd want to carry this kind of baggage into a marriage?!

Unforgiveness

It's said that the first to apologise is the bravest, the first to forgive the strongest and the first to forget the happiest. Forgiveness isn't one of the Ten Commandments. In fact, it's not even something that's talked about very much in sermons but, for all of that, it's one of the most important factors in living healthy and free. Although not a Commandment as such, it is something that is central to enjoying life. Holding grudges makes no one miserable except ourselves, no matter how grievous the hurt, and so the conscious decision to forgive is vital. Forgiving is a decision and not always one we want to take but it's right and necessary. God asks us to: He knows that in forgiving others we release ourselves from bitterness, anger, resentment and retaliation.

Holding on to unforgiveness results in emotional baggage. It leaves us with bitterness, anger, resentment and the wish for retaliation that we mentioned in the last sentence. Obviously we should want to carry as little of this as possible. Emotional baggage always weighs us down, producing not only bitterness but resentment towards those who have hurt us and the world at large. It also makes us angry and, at its extreme, can cause us to make inner vows about what we're going to allow to happen in our lives in future. These vows close us down and can even make us suspicious and mistrustful of our partners.

And here's the rub, those people we hold in unforgiveness often haven't a clue that they've hurt us to the degree they have or that we hold such enmity. They might well be amazed.

The Bible has something to say about unforgiveness. In Mark 11:25[TPT] we're told:

> *"And whenever you stand praying, if you find you carry something in your heart against another person, release him and forgive him so that your Father in heaven will also release you and forgive you of your faults."*

This can be a tall order, and no-one should ever downplay how difficult this can be, but maybe the journey can be made easier if you recognise this: forgiveness starts at home. It has to start with you. We're often our own worst critics. Often the first person we need to forgive is oneself. If we've ever allowed ourselves to have taken responsibility for something that's happened, rightly or wrongly, we can give ourselves a hard time. We can so easily beat ourselves up for not having done enough, or for letting someone else down, or for just failing, without any of this being in anyone else's opinion than our own.

Forgiveness in marriage requires another level of understanding. To quote John Gottman, *"Studies have shown that forgiveness is an essential component of successful romantic relationships. In fact, the capacity to seek and grant forgiveness is one of the most significant factors contributing to marital satisfaction and a lifetime of love."*

Forgiving yourself and others is about being willing to acknowledge that you are capable of being wounded. It also means that you are willing to step out from the role of victim and take charge of your life.

Couples who practice forgiveness can rid themselves of the toxic hurt and shame that holds them back from feeling connected to each other. Emotional attunement is a skill that allows couples to fully process and move on from negative emotional events, and ultimately create a stronger bond. For more on this see our Resources page at the back of this manual.

Sozo Stop:

Father God, am I carrying unforgiveness at the moment about anything?

If so, who do I need to forgive and for what?

Father God, how did all that make me feel?

And then, "Father God, I choose to forgive x for y and these feeling of z that I felt. Father God, I'm not prepared to carry this unforgiveness any longer, will you take it from me?"

And when He does, ask Him what He'd like to give you in return...write this down and discuss with your partner.

Shame

Shame isolates us! It's a hidden secret. It doesn't like coming into the light. It makes us believe that we're constantly uncovered, that the people surrounding us can see all the way into us. It steals our confidence and saps our self-worth. It is the ultimate thief and liar that stops us from being authentic and truly relational. We can take it on ourselves by doing something we consider to be shameful or we can carry shame as a result of what was done to us. Remember that shame, as with anger or divorce or so many repetitive patterns, can be passed down the generations as learned behaviour. Either way, that shame will hold us back from being who Father God wants us to be, a beloved Son or Daughter made in His image living a life knowing who we are and Whose we are, strong in ourselves, known to God and loved by Him. What's more, it will create a barrier or wall between you and your partner if it isn't exposed and dealt with.

We often associate shame with sex but really we can find ourselves ashamed of so much more. It can arise from any activity or thought that we're not proud of, that we wish had never happened, whether done by us or against us. Very often shame comes as a result of having been abused or by allowing sexual sin into our lives. Abuse or sexual sin that has not been dealt with leaves us scarred. We feel dirty, worthless and unlovable, sometimes almost as if we deserved it because possibly we believe we attracted or our wrong doing deserved the abuse. This is a lie! Never take on the responsibility for another person's misbehaviour.

But, if you have acted in a shameful way? What then? Do you feel that your action has placed you beyond God's grace? That He's turned His back on you? The answer is down to you. If a child of yours acted awfully but was truly repentant, how would you respond? Hopefully with an acceptance of them based on your deep love for them. So how much more likely is it that Father God is ready to accept a truly repentant child of His? How much more likely is it that the person you're in love with and intending to marry will understand if you are open, honest and vulnerable. Nothing is beyond redemption with true and full repentance. Whatever you might feel, the truth is that God has forgiven you and you can expect your partner, who truly loves you, to understand and, if necessary, to forgive you too. And if you've been abused and have just read this paragraph, remember that we need to forgive much because we in turn have been forgiven much. It may not be easy, it may well take time, it's definitely a process, and it's a process that can happen once we have come to terms with the abuse and only then through a healing process. It's also a choice, but it's a choice that leads to release and freedom.

Thought Stop!

Is there anything that you feel ashamed about?

Do you know of anything that your partner feels ashamed about?

If I knew my partner had been abused, would I still love them?

Sozo Stop!

Father God, when was the first time I felt shame?

Father God, who do I need to forgive for that shame?

I choose to forgive _____ for _____

Father God, what effect did their actions have on me?

I choose to forgive _____ for the effects their actions have changed my life.

Father God if I hand you shame what do you want to give me instead?

Old Friends

In the chapter on *Living With the Past* we've already considered Soul Ties and looked at how we can carry Pain, Unforgiveness and Shame, the down sides of having had past relationships and the damage that can be left in their wake. What we didn't consider were those past relationships we look back at with affection, even love. Nor did we consider the relationships we have with our friends from work, or the gym, school or college or even church mates. How can those relationships affect our partners?

On the face of it there would appear to be nothing wrong with having long term friends or keeping in touch with old friends, even old boyfriends or girlfriends, but is there really an issue with doing this? The answer is "Yes", if bringing the past into your present is to the detriment of your partner and your relationship with them.

Let's first consider old boy and girl friends.

I (Darrell) can speak from experience. I always felt myself fortunate never to have had any sort of terminal row with a soon-not-to-be-girlfriend, and so managed to maintain a level of friendship and even, in retrospect, closeness with them. To me they were old friends and I still valued them. To my then fiancée, now wife, Anthea, they were old girlfriends. They were never a threat to our relationship…in my opinion. Anthea never viewed them as a threat to our relationship either, but my friendship with them and the way I kept in touch was enough to cause her unease. My reluctance to just drop them as friends despite her unease caused us relationship problems. The truth is that I should have been more considerate and stopped the friendships for the good of our relationship. The further truth is that if those old girlfriends were truly friends they would have understood. More to the point I should have understood that allowing anything at all to get between my partner and I was not showing the love and loyalty that should have been there. It's not that Anthea complained, it's just that I should have been tuned in enough to recognise it wasn't good. I should have recognised there were some soul ties I needed to deal with.

Now how about all those friends from work or the gym, what about them? We would suggest that whichever way you look at it, your new life with your partner is going to look very different to your old life as a bachelor. We've dealt with a lot of this when looking at Boundaries in Chapter Six, but there we were looking at things from the point of view of needing both quality time together and space to do one's own thing. Here we just want to make the point that however much you love your old friends, your partner may not feel the same way about them. Your buddies may not automatically become her buddies, nor hers yours. Part of the fun of becoming a new family is making new, mutual, friends. Some of your old friends may become new friends to you both, but please don't make any demands on your partner that they like your old friends just because you do. You do have to let some old friends go, as you give priority to your relationship together.

▓▓▓ Thought Stop!

Are there any old boyfriends / girlfriends you're still in touch with? How do you feel about them? Why are you still in touch?

Do you know whether your partner has old boyfriends / girlfriends they're still in touch with? If so, how does that make you feel? Why do you think they're still in touch?

How would you like your partner to deal with old boyfriends / girlfriends they're still in touch with? Would you be prepared to do the same?

How important is it to you that your partner accepts your work / gym / college / church friends? Why?

How do you feel about your partner's work / gym / college / church friends? Are they more important to them than yours are to you? If so, how do you handle this?

How would you respond if your partner decided they just didn't like your friends?

How would you partner respond if you decided you just didn't like her friends?

How would you partner respond if you decided you just didn't like his/her friends?

▨▨▨ Sozo Stop!

Father God, are there any insecurities in me that cause me to need to hang on to old friends in an unhealthy way?

_____

_____

_____

_____

(If so) Father God, where do these insecurities come from? Is there someone I need to forgive for these?

I choose to forgive _____ for _____

Father God, what effect did their actions have on me?

_____

_____

_____

_____

I choose to forgive _____ for the effects that their actions have had on my life.

Father God if I hand you these insecurities, what do you want to give me instead?

_____

_____

_____

_____

Chapter Twelve

Families

The old adage about being able to choose your friends but not your family is entirely true. In deciding on your partner you're not only choosing them, you're also taking on their family and that could be just a few people or could be extensive, potentially placing huge pressures on you personally and on your relationship with your partner generally. This will obviously be even more applicable if you're heading into a second marriage and one or other, or both, of you are bringing children with you.

Our intention here is not to flood you with advice but to create an opportunity for conversation around the many pitfalls, but also opportunities, that your new life with each other's families will bring. Having said this there are a few fundamentals that you really have to meet. The first is to honour and support each other at all times. Your family may be hugely important to you, but your new partner should be even more important.

A Biblical marriage is about leaving and cleaving. Even before the Fall, it says in Genesis:

> *"That is why a man leaves his father and mother and is united to his wife, and they become one flesh" (Genesis 2:24).*

The pattern for marriage is that a man and woman leave the family units they have been part of and become a new family. This doesn't mean we don't respect our parents or continue to honour them, but it does mean that together we find a way of being. So many marriages struggle because one of the partners wants to run back to mum or dad and involve them in the disagreement or use them to get their way. When a couple make the vow of faithfulness it includes forsaking all others and this includes letting go of the apron strings of our parents. Whilst a couple may choose together to listen to the wisdom of their parents this has to be a joint choice and not an enforced one. Respecting your parents when you are an adult doesn't necessarily mean obeying them. For parents it means letting go and releasing the couple getting married.

When the Bible talks about leaving and cleaving, it's not just referring to your parents. Like Biblical repentance, it means turning your face entirely the opposite way and recognising that your partner and their family is, to you, your new family. Not that you deny your birth family, but you give your new family equal standing in your life. Can you see how if you both adopt this approach you'll benefit from the best of both families?

Furthermore, whatever your thoughts and opinions about your own parents and family, don't insist that your partner shares them. Let them form their own opinion and live with it. We all have a tendency to want our partners to agree and support our feelings, but our experience is that it's best to let our partners find their own levels. Don't interpret this as them not honouring you. See it as you honouring and trusting them to do the right thing.

A last point before a Thought Stop! It can be difficult if your new partner has children from a previous relationship, especially if you have children of your own. Our top tip is not to rush but to remember that, above all ,your job with your partner's children, whatever their age, is to become someone they can trust as a friend, mentor and supporter. You need them to respect you and appreciate you and that will take time. Leave the discipline to their parent. If you and your partner can work together with this understanding things are likely to go much more smoothly.

Thought Stop!

How does the thought of your partner making friends with your family make you feel?

How do you feel about their family?

What would make getting to feel a part of your partner's family more easy? What would help you getting to feel part of your partner's family?

What will you find difficult about leaving and cleaving?

And if there are children involved:

Did you end up being parented by someone not your birth parent?

What would you change?

How do you feel about parenting someone else's children? What do you see as being the challenges?

How do you think you can work together on this? What support do you need?

███ Sozo Stop!

Father God, do I have any unhealthy ties to my family that I need to break to be able to form this new union?

(If so) Father God, I choose to break any unhealthy ties with my family, and I choose to leave my family and cleave to my new husband/wife.

Father God, are there any areas in which I struggle to honour my new in-laws?

Father God, do I need to forgive my in-laws for anything?

Father God, what tools do you give me to help me honour my in-laws?

STARTING OUT

Chapter Thirteen

Spiritual Life Together

You may be surprised to hear that many couples, if not most, don't pray together. They may share their quiet time, reading their Bibles together or praying individually, but not many actually pray together and that's rather sad. It's also not Kingdom! We make that rather bold claim because, as we've been saying throughout, marriage is about relationship and few things are more intimate and relational than praying together.

But is praying together enough? The answer to that question is going to depend on your individual positions regarding the importance and relevance of the spiritual dimension to your everyday life. Let us explain!

What the acceptance of Jesus looks like in your daily life will differ wildly from person to person. We tend to make an assumption that once we've become Christians we're all basically on the same page and that any differences in beliefs or the way we live our faith won't make a huge difference in the general run of things. This easily translates into the idea that just getting on and loving each other day to day is what matters. This suggests that any differences experienced in our faith and belief won't necessarily matter that much or have any impact on our lives. What we're actually doing here, without necessarily realising it, is making our faith fit into our everyday rather than as it should be, the other way around.

If that's the way you both want to live your life and marriage you can pretty well skip the rest of this Chapter, but if you both want to live your life out of faith rather than fitting it into life, you may want to read on...but first:

Thought Stop!

How important is your faith to you? Think about this carefully before you respond. What would life without Jesus be like?

How important do you think your partner's faith is to them?

Would you like your faith to have a bigger place in your life?

What do you both think about each other's answers and where would you actually like to be?

If you've had that discussion and found that your views on faith and spirituality are wildly different, please don't just brush this disparity under the carpet and press on. Living and being true to your faith should be central to your existence and any compromise to accommodate a partner has to be weighed very carefully. The Biblical reference to being 'equally yoked' (2 Corinthians 6:14) is overused and anyway who even knows how oxen are yoked nowadays. Nevertheless, the underlying truth remains, if you marry someone who does not share your faith you place yourself in a position of compromise, however happy they are for you to get out there and follow your faith. Living your faith on your own will never be entirely fulfilling, however much you try and persuade yourself that it will be.

On top of which, remember this, you are absolutely not responsible for praying/bringing/cajoling your partner to faith. That's Jesus' job, working in their heart, not yours to beat yourself up about. Are we saying that you should never marry someone whose spiritual life isn't the same as yours? No, we're not, but what we are saying is that you both need to recognise the differences and decide to work together to achieve God's desires for you, the desires you might now know from having worked through Chapter 1!

Here's another question for you. Who do you think should be responsible for taking the spiritual lead in your marriage? And before you answer, let me say that it's a bit of a trick question. Ultimately both partners in a marriage are responsible for its spiritual health and for encouraging each other in faith – it's part of being in a Biblical marriage.

Thought Stop!

What do you hope for in your marriage? What would you like your life in Jesus to look like together? How important would praying together be for you?

How can you see the two of you working together to achieve this?

What barriers or obstacles can you see?

Sozo Stop!

Father God, how do you see us?

Father God, can you show me what we need to deal with in our lives that might act as barriers in our relationship with you?

What would our walk with you look like without those barriers?

We're getting you to do a lot of the work in this chapter but it's amazing how, as couples, we commonly discuss our secular lives but fail to talk to each other about our walk with Jesus.

What you'll find as you spend time unpacking this subject together is that each of you will have spiritual strengths that you bring to your relationship. Anthea is an intercessor, has a discerning prophetic ability and loves worship; Darrell has an innately deep and unquestioning faith that is the foundation for their relationship. As each brings out the best in the other, each learns from the other, together they grow, individually and as a couple. Recognising each other's strengths isn't, by default, finding each other's weakness, it's an opportunity to discover how the new mutual support system you're developing is going to work.

This idea of mutual support is inherent in marriage. You could say that in the best of all worlds it's inherent in friendships too. The wording of the marriage ceremony, and this is true wherever you are, leans towards the idea of loving through thick and thin, of supporting each other 'till death do you part'. However, perhaps strangely for a Christian ceremony, this is taken by most people to refer to every day life rather than life in the Spirit. The truth is that the spiritual support you are able to give to each other is more important than any temporal support you can give. All our lives go through 'seasons'. All of us have those times when God seems to be distant or to have given up on us, when praying is a struggle and we wonder if He even exists. It's then that you need to be strong for each other, and then that the stronger of you needs to take a lead in prayer. It's then that you should dig out the prophetic words spoken over you both and use them as declarations of who you are, whose you are and the plans He has for you both!

Sozo Stop!

Father God, what purposes have you for our spiritual life together?

What follows may appear to be the most obvious question for you to discuss together, but we'll give it to you anyway.

How do you want to set the atmosphere in your new home together?

If you haven't read Dawna de Silva's book *Shifting Atmospheres* we recommend it! In essence it tells us that we are at all times living in a spiritual world but that most of us are not tuned into it. We live, breath and see in the natural, but what we're aware of is only a very small part of what there is. The more you learn to see and feel beyond the natural, the more you become aware of the supernatural, and it's in the supernatural that Holy Spirit operates. You'll have heard of those people who can see angels, who pray for healing and it happens and whose prophetic gifting is extraordinary. They're all in tune with the supernatural. You may not be operating at quite that level but all of us are capable of recognising atmospheres. A lot of the time you're doing it without even recognising that you are. Have you ever worked somewhere and had a toxic workmate or boss? Someone who only has to enter the room for the atmosphere to change. You may not have thought of it as such, but you're feeling that atmosphere supernaturally, it's not something that can be explained by science.

Getting back to the question, you can change and determine the atmosphere your home will carry. We once had a complete stranger in our house and within about five minutes she asked if we were Christians. We told her we were and asked how she knew. "I can sense the atmosphere of peace", she replied. If your home hasn't got Jesus at its centre it won't be peaceful, physically or spiritually. If your home is a place where the fruit of the spirit are manifest it will be happy and welcoming. In contrast, if it is a home where anger, tension, bitterness and unhealthy ways of relating occur regularly it will not feel happy or welcoming for you or your visitors.

Thought Stop!

What do you want the atmosphere in your new home together to be like?

What steps will you take together to ensure that's what happens?

Sozo Stop!

Father God, is there any area of my life in which I have come under an unGodly atmosphere or partnered with an ungodly atmosphere?

_____

_____

_____

_____

Father God, is there anyone I need to forgive for learning this ungodly atmosphere was normal?

_____

_____

_____

_____

Father God, I choose to dismantle my listening ears to the voice of the atmosphere of _____ and I ask you to retune my ears to hear your broadcast instead. Father God, what is the atmosphere you want me to partner with?

_____

_____

_____

_____

Chapter Fourteen

Good Vibrations, the Art of Communications

Yes, you're right, we've touched on the area of communications before. That was really more to do with the misunderstandings and misconceptions that can so easily happen between even the most loving of couples, causing miscommunication and unhappiness. Let's now spend just a little time thinking about how, as a couple, you can ensure that your communications speak to each other…

You'll no doubt know the old phrase, 'Do as you would be done by'. You do? Well, it's misleading! You might like to be showered with presents and told you're wonderful. Your partner, on the other hand, may be completely untouched by presents and kind words but will feel deeply loved when you give them a hug and make them a cup of tea or coffee. This old saying would be better rendered as, 'Do as they would be done by'. In other words, try and understand how to communicate in your partner's language and not your own. If your partner's primary love language is acts of service you need to communicate your love to them by doing things for them, whether or not this is also your primary love language doesn't matter.

If you feel that we've said that before we make no apology, it's one of the failings we see most often and it happens because we forget or, more to the point, we forget to make the effort.

Here's a question for you: how many different types of communication are there?

Actually, it's a question that carries a much bigger answer than you might imagine. The study of anthroposemiotics, human communications, fills a great deal more shelf space than most libraries have room for. Our ability as humans to communicate verbally and to transmit and receive complex understandable thoughts, responses and emotions is what distinguishes us from animals. It's a subject of great interest and scrutiny but all we need to know is that those elements of communication that are important to a marriage can be slimmed down to verbal and non-verbal, with writing thrown in as a very valuable extra (remember letters?).

There's an often misquoted study by Mehrabian and Ferris which states that in the business of verbal communications, the actual words you use only constitute 7% of the message conveyed. Although it's a misquote it does point to something important. The way you say things, the clarity of your speech, its modulation, pitch, volume and speed all convey meaning, as do the non-verbal elements such as body language and visual cues. We don't even think of most of these things when we're engaged in conversation. We just do what comes naturally but what for us comes naturally is very often a replication of the mannerisms and speech patterns we've learned from our parents.

This can be fine if we've been brought up in a home where Dad honoured Mum and vice versa, where both spoke respectfully to each other and purposefully listened to what each other had to say, because if this is the case then we have a head start toward being the same. If not, and home was a constant shouting match then we may have a lot to learn. We will have no-one to learn it from other than our partner who, after all, is probably the best person to teach us if, and it's a big if, we're prepared to accept the need to change.

Thought Stop!

How would you describe the type of communication you grew up with?

How did it affect your parents?

How do or did your partner's parents relate to each other?

Can you see any similarity in the way that you communicate with your partner?

Can you see any similarity in the way that your partner communicates with you?

Is there anything you've identified that you'd like to change in how you communicate with each other?

Communications Workout!

In a Biblical marriage do you think that the both of you should be happy for each other to be lovingly powerful and assertive in your dealings with each other? Are there situations when you feel it would be OK to be verbally passive or verbally aggressive with each other? Do you think you should speak up to your partner in a child to parent way, or down to your partner as a parent does to a child, or across as adult to adult? And how would being at the receiving end of each of these make you feel?

Hopefully your answer will be that you'd like your partner to be loving, to be powerful and to speak to you as one adult to another without being either passive or aggressive.

Here's why. We communicate in different ways. Option one, when I communicate with you passively, never appearing to have any need or thought of my own, I'm not really being honest with you or myself. I'm saying "You matter and I don't" or, to put it another way, it's too much bother to communicate to you what I really think or need. In truth what's happening is that I'm hiding my thoughts and emotions behind a facade because I'm not used to expressing myself or I'm afraid of what will happen and what you will think if I'm open and let you see the real me. At best this attitude is expressing a wish to please one's partner at all costs. At worst it's evidence of deep emotional hurt that's making the person concerned need to hide what's really going on inside them.

Option two, when I communicate with you aggressively, always having to make a point, win an argument and get my own way I'm inherently saying, "I matter, you don't" or "I need to be in control to feel secure in myself". Perhaps, oddly, this response to life and relationship is usually fear based too, in that aggression is usually covering up an insecurity or an unwillingness or inability to let people see what's really going on inside. It's a bully tactic based on the idea that if I can get one over on you before you get one over on me, then I can control the situation and not risk being exposed. If you're a naturally passive person yourself you might feel, at least for a time, that you're being protected by a verbally aggressive partner. Believe us, ultimately, you're really not.

The truth is that there will be a time when you will want to express your needs and not want to be dependent on your partner. When this happens, your partner will struggle to change the pattern that's been working for you both and your relationship may then struggle to find a new normal.

Option three is the one we didn't mention above but is really the worst of all worlds. If I'm acting passive-aggressively because of my own powerlessness, appearing to be loving on the surface but with every comment being barbed and hurtful then my message is, "You matter – Not!" Passive-aggressive behaviour can be so insidious, so subtle that at first it's easy to think that it's your own fault that you're hearing what your partner is saying in such a negative way. There'll be comments that sound caring but have hidden meaning, innuendo that carries unkindness, sarcasm that isn't funny, the use of silence to hurt, all manipulative, all aimed to control and belittle, all aimed at making you feel that whatever is going on is your fault. If this is you then inner healing will help to overcome the feelings of powerlessness that have led to this damaging way of doing life

On the other hand, Option four, assertive communication says, "You matter, and so do I". It says that you're important and need to be thought about, loved and cherished and so do I. It's the language of mutual respect, care and love. It's what you want to aim for in your relationship.

Thought Stop!

Which of these four options do you easily recognise? Can you think of examples of each amongst the people you know? How do you feel when you're with that person?

Do you recognise that you use any of these four options yourself? Which do you use the most? What is it that leads you to use a healthier or less healthy option?

Do you recognise any of these four options in your partner? Which one do they use most of the time? What happens in life to lead them to use a healthier or less healthy option?

How do you think you both need to change? What can your contribution to change be? What can you do that might help your partner to change things they want to?

Practical Communications

Moving on from the theory. In any relationship there are three distinct levels of communication. Every relationship needs each of these levels to be engaged regularly to make it feel complete and fulfilling and for the couple to feel fully connected with each other. These three levels are 'informational', 'intermediate' and 'inspirational'.

Informational is the type of communication that most of us do on a daily basis. We tell our partner when we are going to work, we chat about who needs to pick up the kids or put out the bins. It's the day-in day-out conversation that makes up a lot of what we say. Informational conversation is important for the communication and exchange of information but doesn't do much to connect us on a deeper emotional level. Going back to Chapter One and the subject of Purpose, this is the type of conversation that we would use when fulfilling the tactics of our lives, the day to day strategies we employ to get from one end of the day to the other.

Intermediate communication is more about what we might be thinking or planning in the next six months or year. It will be about the holidays we're going to take, our plans for work and how to manage our money from month to month. It's the more important conversations about the bigger issues rather than about the day to day things. These conversations do involve relating at a more emotional level as it involves your shared interests, but they are primarily to do with practical things in life.

Inspirational communication meets our deeper need to be heard and understood. It involves relating at the emotional level. At this level of communication we speak about our hopes and dreams, our deep thoughts and about feelings and issues. We listen to our partner and reflect on their thoughts. Understanding one's partner at this deeper level will affect the choices we make at the intermediate and informational levels of communication. This is where we are vulnerable and open. Asking questions like "Where would you like to be in five years?" and "What would you do with a £/$1m?" can help this communication. "What do you feel about this?", "Does this make you feel excited or scared?", "How would you like me to support you emotionally in this?", "Shall we pray about this together?' The inspirational level of communication goes beyond a business type relationship to one of deep emotional and spiritual intimacy.

Can you see how making a point of engaging in all three levels of communication, especially the Inspirational, which probably won't come as naturally as the other two, can help to draw you closer?

Thought Stop!

Can you identify if you do all three types of communication as a couple? When do you do them?

What would help improve the depth of communication you have at all levels?

What would help you to feel more listened to at each level?

What can you do to improve your communication with each other?

Thoughtful Communication

So far in this chapter we've mostly dealt with the spoken element of communication, how to present the words we use with each other. What about the non-verbal? What do you understand by the term 'love languages'? In a nutshell these 'languages', defined by their originator, Gary Chapman, in his 1992 book, *The Five Love Languages,* are a way of looking at how we give and receive love. The idea behind them is that if we don't receive love in our love language then we will feel unloved, even if the person loves us. It's worth saying that you'll often be able to recognise a person's love language by the way they act towards you, if your partner is constantly doing things for you or buying you presents you might find that these are their love languages even if they're not yours.

The five love languages are Quality Time, Touch, Gifts, Acts of Service and Words of Affirmation.

Quality time – this isn't just spending time with someone but really focusing on that person. It isn't about what we do but the fact we are actively choosing to be with them and nothing else. If this isn't one of your languages but it is your partner's you might think that watching TV together or even talking in the car is spending quality time together. It isn't, it's just spending time. Focusing on someone, even if you love them, may not come naturally to you. Learning how to immerse yourself in what they're telling you, verbally and non-verbally will always be worth it. Here's the good news, giving quality time to someone doesn't have to occupy your every waking moment. Just make sure that your quality time partner feels loved and listened to constantly…or at least regularly once or twice a day.

Touch – physical touch, and we're not (necessarily) talking about sex here. You'll know if you or your partner are 'touch' people because you'll be always reaching out to hold a hand, rub an arm or give a hug. Hugs are the most natural thing in the world for a touch person. Even sitting close can speak volumes to them! Massage their feet, caress their hair, touch their shoulder, it's non-verbal communication at its best!

Gifts – it doesn't have to be a big thing. It can be a little present that means such a lot, especially if it's been thought through and beautifully wrapped! If you're not a gifts person you'll find it hard to understand the impact and flood of love that even the simplest but considered gift can provoke with someone who feels loved by such things. It doesn't mean that they're materialistic, it just means that they recognise love in the gift of thought and care that's gone into a gift from you.

Acts of Service – this is any practical way that one of you serves the other, from making a cup of tea to doing jobs around the house. Filling the car with fuel, emptying the rubbish, making sure there's always milk in the fridge, picking up your own clothes, or theirs, these are all small acts of service that will tell your partner that you're thinking of them and that they're important to you. Actually, clearing up after yourself will be particularly important if this is your partner's love language.

Words of Affirmation – these are all those words that can mean so much. The person who has this as their Love Language needs to hear how much they mean to you. Telling them they've done a good job, that they look beautiful/handsome, that their efforts at gardening are stunning, or just that you love them and you're proud of being with them, these are all affirming and will make your partner feel loved and wanted.

Is that it? No, it isn't, because there something you really need to be aware of when it comes to love languages. Denying these or acting in an opposite way can cause huge distress! If your partner's love language is Affirmation and you make a cutting comment or are aggressive and rude to him/her, such nastiness will feel like a knife in the back. If it's Touch and you, heaven forbid, hit them the emotional hurt will be far greater than the physical pain. And, back to an earlier point, if it's Acts of Service and you refuse to tidy up or lift a finger to help, then that will soon cause a serious rift.

'Success' in communication is not just to have your words understood and your emotions interpreted, it's also that you understand your partner's words and emotions. There's a postcard that has on it the phrase, 'Love is understanding every word your partner doesn't say' and never was a truer word spoken in jest.

Thought Stop!

What is your primary love language?

What is your partner's primary love language?

What do you already do that speaks to your partner's language?

And what do they do that speaks to your primary language?

What more could you do to make your partner feel more loved?

What more could your partner do to make you feel loved?

Sozo Stop!

Jesus, is there anything I need to forgive my partner for in the area of communication?

Jesus, is there anything I need to ask forgiveness for?

Jesus, where did I learn passive/ aggressive patterns of communication?

Jesus, I forgive _____ for teaching me this pattern of communication and for the effect it's had on my life.

Jesus, what lie have I believed about communication?

Jesus, what's the truth and how will this affect our relationship?

Chapter Fifteen

Sex!

This could have been either a very long chapter or a surprisingly short one. We've touched on the subject of sex a few times already but whilst we've talked about being open and honest about our pasts and being prepared to be vulnerable about our desires there's potentially a lot more to discuss together. For example, what is healthy sex in marriage? This is a great question, as is what is the role of sex in marriage? How about one of you refusing the other? Is that allowed? And what are the limits? And how about contraception?

You might think that the answers to these and most other questions about sex should be pretty obvious but the fact that Agony Aunts across the globe are making a living from answering questions from embarrassed and anonymous correspondents would suggest otherwise. So, what is healthy sex exactly? What is 'enough'?

It might surprise you that we'd suggest that these are the wrong questions to be asking at this point in the conversation. Let's instead start with the role of sex in marriage. Shouldn't the why come before the how often? When those extraordinary fathers of the Faith who wrote the Bible were trying to articulate the very closest of all close relationships to exemplify God's love for us, they chose the intimacy between lovers as their model. When enjoyed by two people committed to each other in marriage, the physical blending of their two bodies is the strongest statement that we possess of what love is …it is the personification of a healthy marriage, so how important is it? Very. Is it the most important thing in a marriage? It shouldn't be. Sex may be the icing on the cake but if that cake doesn't have all the right ingredients, mixed together correctly and cooked to perfection then no amount of icing will hide the fact that it's not a good cake.

Sex in marriage is deeply important. Intimacy, whether physical, emotional or spiritual is even more important. If your intimacy leads to sex, wonderful, but intimacy can be expressed and enjoyed in other ways. These ways can also be physical, but there are ways that can express love and tenderness that are not remotely physical. If you both make it into your 80s and beyond, you'll very likely experience the truth of this! Knowing this and maintaining intimacy with your partner and honouring them at all times in your marriage will lead to all those other questions being resolved. So, what is healthy sex? It's whatever gives both of you pleasure whilst honouring each other's wishes and desires. What is 'enough'? It's whatever gives both of you pleasure whilst honouring each other's wishes and desires. You get the picture.

Potentially more difficult is how you deal with mismatched needs. Stop right there! Are we talking here about needs or desires or expectations or even requirements, because each of these carries its own atmosphere. And are we talking about sex? You immediately thought we were, didn't you, but go back to the last paragraph, the most important thing in marriage is intimacy. Marriage doesn't give you a right to have sex. It gives you the expectation that your partner who loves you will want to be intimate with you, whatever that looks like and they will expect that from you in equal measure. You may have an equal need, desire, expectation or requirement for sex but if not then it will be the depth of intimacy and love you have for each other that will enable you both to arrive at the sweet spot that satisfies you both.

Does this make sense to you both? Does it explain why questions about limits and what's allowed fall away when an intimacy born from mutual honour and respect are paramount?

Having said all that, where do you get help if it doesn't work and sex is not great?

Like all areas of marriage, sex takes practice and not every couple has amazing sex from day one. In fact, it's probably important to create some realistic expectations in this area, recognising that it can take time to get to know each other physically. Most couples, with time and practice, will find ways to make this an enjoyable part of their marriage. For some couples it remains a difficult area. The most important thing is not to let your upset about it cause embarrassment between you or, even worse, start the blame game. Talk about it openly with each other, without blaming. Find ways to reassure and reaffirm your love for each other and to enjoy intimacy in other ways until this becomes a fulfilling area for you. If you as a couple experience ongoing difficulty with sex once you're married we would advise finding a mature couple who are experienced at giving advice in this area, or a counsellor who deals with sexual issues in marriage to help you. Don't give up hope because, whatever the obstacle, with the proper help it can be overcome.

Thought Stop!

How important do you think sex will be in your marriage?

How will you cope if you have different levels of sex drive?

Is it OK for one of you to refuse the other sexually?

Do you think sex is vital for intimacy?

What limits would you place on your sexual activity? Are you happy with sex toys, fantasy etc.?

Whose responsibility is contraception?

What are your thoughts about which form of contraception to use? Why?

Sozo Stop!

Father God, have I believed any lies about the role of sex in marriage or my expectations of sex?

Father God, where did I learn these lies or expectations?

Father God, who do I need to forgive?

_____

_____

_____

_____

Father God, I forgive _____ for _____

Father, I renounce the lie _____

Father God, what truth do you want me to know about sex in our marriage?

_____

_____

_____

_____

Chapter Sixteen

Confrontation and Conflict

"Conflict? What conflict? We love each other, we never argue, we get on too well."

Is that you? Is that true?

Can it be?

The answer to that is "Yes!" it can be true! Most of us have known at least one couple who deny ever having had an argument in all their years of marriage, and who are we to doubt the truth of that. The strength of a marriage, though, is not related to how often you argue but how good you are at resolving your differences. People who never argue may actually be failing to resolve the issues between them and be pretending that these issues do not exist. So, let's assume for a moment, perish the thought, that there may on occasion be reason for a temporary disagreement between you. How are you going to handle that? The better prepared you are, the easier it will be to get through it and come out the other side without having caused damage to your relationship.

Here's a pointer to how to manage conflict: there's a difference, a big difference, between conflict and confrontation. You really want to try and avoid going from confrontation, when something has to be said because you're in disagreement with your partner, to conflict, when you're prepared to fight to be right.

There's a simple key to resolving conflict and it's this: keep talking. Keep talking and remember that, whatever is going on, the relationship is more important than the issue. Choose to put valuing your partner above your need to be right or to win. The issue will be resolved and pass, the relationship has to remain. Having said that, perhaps even more important than keeping talking is to keep listening. Confrontation happens when one of you has a requirement or need that is not being addressed or respected by the other. To resolve a confrontation before it turns into a conflict requires both of you to be prepared to listen to each other and to accept that there can be no winner and loser between you. It's not a football game. You both have to be winners. You both need to be happy with the settlement you arrive at. You need to resolve the issue not just at the practical level, but also so you are both emotionally happy with the outcome. You also need to do this without pointing a finger of blame.

A good starting point is not to accuse. "You make me feel…" is blaming. "I feel that…" isn't. Your job is to express yourself and, as we said above, to articulate your requirement and need in a way that can be understood by your partner. You're not challenging them by doing this and you're not responsible for your partner's response, remember that in a relationship you're allowed to think differently and hold different opinions. It should be possible to explore each other's points of view in a safe way.

Here are our top tips for dealing with confrontation and conflict. Use them wisely and prepare to be amazed at how even when confrontation slips into conflict things can be worked out between you.

- Never argue in public. Those around you will remember your disagreement long after you've forgotten it and may well form a judgement about you and your relationship whilst they're at it. Arguing in public might be a way to recruit people onto your side but it won't help your relationship if you belittle your partner in front of others.

- Call a truce. There are times when you just have to agree to disagree and the sooner you get to this point the better for both of you. Why not set a time or go out for a coffee when you're both feeling calm to discuss whatever it is in a less confrontational way? Sometimes in the heat of the moment something can seem really important, but when we go away and think about it, we realise that we have been reacting in an unhelpful way or it isn't really that important after all.

- Reaffirm your commitment to each other. Hopefully you're together because you love each other, so before settling down to discuss the problem it might be a good idea to remind yourself and each other of this. It will help in defusing any heat between you. Gottman, whom we mentioned in a previous chapter, talked about one of the keys of a healthy relationship being when we turn to each other in disagreements rather than away from each other. If your tendency is to run to the cave when you disagree then learning to reaffirm your relationship could be the thing that saves it! Think of the issue as being one that you are both facing together, rather than one that is separating you.

- Be willing to listen. Remember the two ears, one mouth lesson! You should listen twice as much as you should speak. Many people are thinking about what they want to say when their partner is talking and so are not really listening. A good way to show that you have been listening is to reflect back to your partner. For example, "I hear you are saying …………. is that correct?" This way we let our partner know we actually care about what they are saying! If we can show our partner that we understand both their point of view and emotional response to something, the heat will go out of the situation, even if you continue to disagree about it.

- Be willing to talk. And before you point out that this contradicts the point just made, what we mean here is that it's important to be willing to open up, be vulnerable and ready to express your heart when it's time to do so. Very often this is harder for men than women but let's be open handed and just say that what follows is aimed at anyone who finds it hard to express their emotions and feelings.

- Sometimes you just have to be honest with what you're feeling, even though expressing it is really difficult. Sweeping things under the carpet to keep the peace may be a short or even medium-term solution, but it's not being honest to either of you. On the one hand your partner should be the easiest person in the world to talk to, on the other hand they can sometimes be the most difficult. The more you can make openness part of the every day of who you are with each other, the easier life will become.

- Always deal with the issue, not the person. Finding fault with each other undermines your relationship and potentially raises questions as to whether you should actually be together. Avoid attacking the other person as a means of defence.

- Think about how you say things. If you are accusatory when you talk you will find it escalates the disagreement. Using "I" statements that keep the focus on how you feel and taking responsibility for your feelings can be more helpful than the accusatory "You". Let us explain! Pointing the finger at your partner, let alone anyone else, is never going to be a recipe for a peaceful resolution of a problem. How, then, do you let your partner know how their actions are affecting you? It's not by saying, for example, "I feel you are criticising me", because that's still an accusation, but it is by saying, "I feel squashed, that there's nothing I do that's right." Can you see the difference? admitting that you feel squashed is being open with your emotions, it's an honest response that begs an honest response…above all, it's not confrontational.

- Be willing to be the first to say you're sorry but not in such a way as your partner doesn't believe you! Note that we're not saying to be prepared to be the first to say you're sorry because that suggests that it's important to reach a peaceful outcome at all costs. That's not the case. If peace is the product of unhealthy compromise then it won't last; peace has to be the product of mutual agreement. What we're really saying here is that the love you have between you should allow you to say that you're sorry more easily, and to mean it!

- Don't press the 'red hot' buttons! We all have issues that are sensitive for us, and if they are brought up will escalate the argument. Often we choose to bring these up when we feel we are losing or want to distract from our own issues. The problem is that escalating things is never a good long-term tactic. Saying to our partner things like, "You always…." will only ever cause more distress and mean you have more hurt to unpick when everything calms down.

- Be willing to forgive and forget. Once whatever has caused division has been dealt with, it's done. If you feel the need to rake it up again then the forgiveness hasn't been complete. You may need to examine your heart and feelings to see what lie you are believing that holds you in that place.

- Be willing to get outside help. Sometimes a third party has a broader view or can see the wood for the trees. Sometimes their experience is greater than yours: whatever the reason, don't feel shy in asking for help. We may need to swallow our pride and embarrassment and talk about personal and vulnerable things. We need to remember to put our relationship above our personal issues and fear of being vulnerable. There's a caveat though, you have to mutually agree on the third party, and they have to be non-partisan, you can't allow them to take sides.

Thought Stop!

How did you see arguments being resolved in your childhood? How did they make you feel? What effect did they have on you? If you never saw arguments as a child, or never saw them being resolved, what effect has this had on you?

Do you think that confrontation should be avoided at all costs?

Do you feel able to be open and vulnerable with your partner? Is your partner able to be open and vulnerable with you?

If you have an issue with your partner how would you like to resolve it? Would you be able to talk about it without either of you getting upset or even angry or withdrawing?

Are you happy for your partner to raise an issue with you that they would like to resolve? Are you able to avoid feeling put upon and defensive?

Sozo Stop!

Father God, is there anything I need to forgive my parents for in teaching me poor ways to deal with conflict?

Father God, has my parents' behaviour affected how I see confrontation? How?

Father, is there a lie I have believed?

Father God, I ask you to change the way I have viewed confrontation. I choose to give you the wrong way I have viewed confrontation (as fearful, passive aggressive) and I ask you to give me a new, right way of seeing confrontation.

Father God, please show me how you want me to behave and walk in this area. (Listen for His response.)

Father God, is there anything I need to forgive my partner for?

_____

I choose to forgive _____ for _____

Father God, what's the truth that you want me to know?

_____

_____

_____

_____

You don't have to wait until there's problem to have a *Sozo for Couples*! In fact, we'd suggest that every couple should have one as soon as they've decided they have a future together. You'll find details at www.sozoforcouples.org.

STARTING OUT

Chapter Seventeen

Time Together, Time Apart

Most of us have heard some variation or other of the truth that no-one (OK, no-one in their right mind) gets to the end of their life and wishes they had spent more time working. The things that matter most to us usually revolve around our purpose, passions and family and it's these things that should and will demand our time.

AND

For those reading this whose purpose involves Church, now is probably a good time to add this reminder: when it comes to an order of importance for allocating time it is always God first, family second and ministry third. Anyone who has a parent in ministry will know the importance of this simple rule and the need for it to be restated at every opportunity!

Back to the point…in Chapter Six we spoke about Boundaries and the need to respect these with each other. In this Chapter we're going to look at how these apply specifically to time and how expectations around time need to be discussed and understood by both of you.

Of course, it might be that you're both deeply gregarious and know that the delight you have in each other's company is something that will last forever. Several couples we know are absolutely inseparable and share everything. Neither would dream of doing anything without the other and to all intents they are perfect partners on every level. If this sounds like it could be you then, "Lucky you!"

Or is it?

Is there, potentially, something not quite right about living in each other's pocket all the time? Could this, maybe, become a foundation for a damaging co-dependency where you just cannot do life without each other where if, heaven forbid, something happens to one of you, the other person of you will just crumble?

You may want to think about that for a moment. On the other hand, you may also think that we're busy encouraging you to have an independent spirit. We're really not. But what we are encouraging is an honesty about your own needs. We'll talk about the constraints of having to work for a living later but here's the thing, it's not unloving to want time on your own. It is also not a demonstration of a lack of love if you want to continue one or more of the hobbies or activities you've enjoyed up until now. Now, if you're obsessive about whatever it is and want to spend your every free moment doing it that's very different. We're assuming that you developed a life and interests before you met your partner and that you'd like the love you have between you to add to the fullness of your life, rather than detract from it. All this is to say that now would be a good time to talk to each other about your expectations of the time and times you'll spend together. It would be great if you shared a love for motor racing, sailing or model railways. However, if you don't, you need to give each other permission to continue with their interests but within the boundaries you agree between the two of you for each other.

Of course, time on your own doesn't need to be anything to do with hobbies. If one, or both of you are introverts you'll need you-time and that should be fine. If you're not an introvert and have limited experience of living with one you might find it difficult to understand their need to be given space to be alone. Believe us when we tell you that it's real and needs to be honoured. Introverts, and especially outgoing introverts can manage in company to a point and then they just need to go away and let life continue without them for a time, and you have to factor this into the way you do life together. It's not uncommon for an introvert to be in a relationship with an extravert. They will need to discuss and agree how they can both have their need for time alone and social time met, and in doing so recognise the validity of these needs.

Thought Stop!

Would you consider yourself an introvert, an outgoing introvert or an extrovert?

What do you think your partner is?

What would you consider your hobbies and interests to be?

What do you know of your partner's hobbies and interests?

How much time do your hobbies and interests take up? How much would you be prepared to give up for the sake of your relationship?

How much alone time do you need every day / week?

So far in this Chapter we've only talked about life for the two of you as a couple. And we haven't yet mentioned the subject of work or babies. What happens when you're both devoting a lot of time to your careers. What happens when baby comes along?

You'll have heard of the work/life balance. Try Googling it and you'll find more tips about managing your work/life balance than you can shake a stick at. None of them appear to suggest the most obvious starting point. Reverse the order. It should be a life/work balance, because it's hard for any relationship to survive one of you, or even both of you having a live-to-work mentality. Of course, you have to make a living but remember the reminder at the beginning of this Chapter for those in ministry, God first, then family, then ministry, except if you're not in ministry it's God first, then family then work!

Thought Stop!

How important is work and career to you?

How important do you think work/career is to your partner?

How do your answers above fit in with the God first, family / marriage second, and work third model?

Babies? We'll talk about them in another chapter but even without children your relationship is going to be pretty full. We suggest that any busy relationship needs the help of a bit of planning and forethought to make sure your need for time together is met. Very often a couple will think that because they live together and see each other at some point during the day they're doing everything needed to keep their relationship sweet. They're usually not and it's those couples who one day find that they've drifted apart. They haven't been working on the togetherness of their relationship, they've taken it and each other for granted.

What's the answer?

For any existing couple we reckon there's four types of time you should consider:

A. You (as a couple) time. Just the two of you, together. Sharing a meal, watching a film, going on a car journey. This is quality time for each other. This is where you spend time talking and asking those inspirational meaningful questions!

B. Time spent together or together with others. Working on something together, out for a meal with friends. This is still relationship building time and may be when you do some of that intermediate communication.

C. Time spent close, but not together. You're on the laptop, your partner is reading or watching TV. They're busy cooking, you're playing with the cat.

D. Time spent apart. You're at work, your partner's at work. You're not, they are. You get the picture.

Thought Stop!

How comfortable are you with the time you spend together at the moment?

Do you think it's enough? Is it the right balance of the different types of time as expressed above?

Does your partner think you spend enough time together? What do you think they would say about the time balance you have?

How do you think your time balance could be improved in a way that works for you both?

In case you're wondering whether there's a norm or suggested norm for how much time a couple should find for each other we would suggest that in a typical week a couple should find the time to have:

A.   One or two 'sessions' (a session being a morning, afternoon or evening) of 'A' time – quality time spent together

B.   Three to four sessions spent together or with friends working on something or out for a meal

C.   Four to eight sessions spent close but not necessarily together.

D.   The rest of the week is usually work or doing whatever else you have to do.

Sozo Stop!

Father God, how do you see my need for "me-time", or my need to be around people all the time? Is there something I need to change?

Chapter Eighteen

Children

Role models are usually thought of as being 'good things', people we point to with gratitude for what they've taught us and modelled to us. It would be wonderful if all our role models were positive, but sadly this is rarely the case, sometimes the people we've learned from and base our behaviour on can be responsible for us learning bad or unhelpful practices. The more we're aware of the influence that role models have had on us and the way we think, the easier it is for us to accept that there may be other better ways of thinking and doing life.

For most of us the most influential role models in our lives will have been our parents. Whether the experience of growing up was happy or horrendous it will probably have left us with deep convictions as to how we want to bring up our own children, and if your conviction differs from your partner's then disagreements are just waiting to happen. It's so important that you agree how you're going to bring your children up in advance.

A united front in parenting is central to a happy childhood. Stability and love are any child's greatest need. The less children see any evidence of unhealthy disagreement and upset between you the happier and more stable they will be. If you take nothing else away from this chapter make it that you should never ever have any unhealthy confrontations in front of children that don't get resolved. You're stealing a bit of their childhood every time you do. To demonstrate to your children that you can have a confrontation and resolve it and continue to love each other is positive modelling. To never resolve a confrontation in their presence means they will fear confrontation and avoid it in later life.

How you answer these next Thought Stops and the discussions you'll have together as a result should act as the foundation for the way you 'do' children going forward..

Thought Stop!

Do you want children / more children? If so, how many?

Do you feel your own childhood was happy and that it set you up for adulthood?

Did your parents allow you to sort out your own problems or did they tell you what to do? Did they rescue you when things went wrong?

Did your parents model an ability to resolve issues and confrontations between them? Was this helpful or unhelpful for you?

What model of discipline did your parents use? Did it work with you? Would you want to use the same model with your children?

Did your parents use punishment to try and control you? Did they encourage you to take responsibility for the problems you caused? How can you combine discipline with grace?

What do you know about your partner's parents and their way of bringing up their children?

As you think about having children, what would you say is the purpose of parenting? The answer to this question may not be as obvious as you originally thought. Some may say that it's to create a loving atmosphere for children to grow in, others to help children be happy. Others again will tell you that the purpose of parenting is to prepare children for life in the real world as adults. What do the two of you think?

Whatever your answer, the truth is that your motivation in having children and the purpose you think parenting has will influence the way you parent, as will, of course, your own experiences of being parented. Understanding these two things is vital.

So, let's look at how you were parented. The Thought Stop questions will have got you talking about this. Hopefully there will be some things from your own experience that you would like to apply to your own parenting and some things you'd like to change. Bear in mind that making changes is not being disrespectful of your parents, but rather learning from their mistakes and challenges. It seems obvious to say it, but if your experience of childhood was painful the key is not to repeat the same pattern with your own children. And if you still carry the pain, may we encourage you to have a Sozo? It's an irony that we are more likely to repeat the mistakes and behaviour of our parents if we have not dealt with the pain than if we do. Dealing with that pain allows us to make new choices and to learn healthier parenting tools.

Back to the purpose of parenting. If your answer was to make our children happy, then how do you respond when they want the latest new toy and tell you that their happiness depends on it. If we don't get them that toy or the budget doesn't stretch that far…are we failing them?

The reality is that no parent can make a child happy, or to put it differently, happiness can be the by-product of healthy relationships, but it does not serve us well as a goal in itself.

Consider this: Proverbs 22:6[NIV] tells us to

> *"Direct your children onto the right path, and when they are older, they will not leave it."*

As parents our role is to help our children prepare for life in the world, to know the path to follow and to call out the destiny over their lives. We live in a world that offers lots of choices and we need to create an environment where children learn to make good, healthy choices as well as how to respond and deal with mistakes. If we try to control everything they do, then that can lead to them not learning enough in a safe home environment about how to manage freedom well. If we go to the other extreme and allow them freedom in every area of their lives before they can understand the consequences of their decisions, then they won't understand boundaries and responsibility. Creating a loving, safe environment where our children learn to manage freedom with responsibility should be our prime objective. We want them to grow into healthy adults who make positive choices.

What does creating that environment look like in practice?

We'd suggest that instead of trying to control everything our children watch, read and surf, we teach them to discern for themselves what is appropriate and what isn't. For a three-year-old this might look like teaching them that the cartoon with fighting in it may make them want to hit their siblings, whilst another programme will make them feel peaceful. For a fourteen-year-old it would be helping them to understand that whilst they can click on any link on the computer, not all of them will lead to good websites.

This way of parenting means that we have to talk to and connect with our children. We have to help them be reflective and then proactive. It means that instead of using our parental 'power' to rule the roost we use it to help our children become powerful and free. Anyone who has been a parent will tell you that trying to control your children doesn't work well and can lead to many arguments. Instead, teaching your children to take responsibility in a way that suits their age can facilitate them growing into mature adults. For example, instead of shouting at a child for not tidying their room (or indeed just leaving it and avoiding going into it) would it be better to give them a choice. "Do you want to tidy your room or give me your pocket money this week and I'll do it for you" can be empowering for both you and them. When they realise that they don't have the money to buy that much coveted toy, then suddenly cleaning their room doesn't seem such a price to pay!

A great resource that unpacks this kind of parenting further is *Loving Your Kids On Purpose* by Danny Silk and we would recommend you read this before having children.

Here are some more things to think about and discuss:

Thought Stop!

How will you handle infertility? It happens in about 20% of couples and can cause huge anxiety and unhappiness. What's your response to this possibility? Would you consider IVF, infertility treatment or adoption?

How would you feel about an unplanned pregnancy? How would you handle it as a couple?

If a scan showed your baby was going to be disabled, how would you cope with that as a couple?

Would you ever consider adoption? If so, what could that look like for you? Why?

There's another set of considerations for you to discuss, especially if you're going to be a blended family. How are you going to manage that? What will the family look like? How will you achieve integration?

We spoke a little about this in Chapter Twelve. To save you having to flick back, this was the question:

How does one respond if your new partner has children from a previous relationship? This is always tough, especially if you have children of your own. Our top tip is not to rush but to remember that above all your job with your partner's children, whatever their age, is to become someone they can trust as a friend, mentor and supporter. You need them to respect you and appreciate you and it will take time. At least at the outset leave the discipline to their parent. There's no rush for you to stamp your authority. If you and your partner can work together with this understanding things will go much more smoothly. A friend, commenting on this, told me;

"My own personal experience is that my husband was a widower when we married and his two children of 6yrs and 9yrs old were very much part of the package! Whilst I never set out to replace their mother, I have fulfilled that role and they see me as their mother and the grandmother to their children, they are very much my children and grandchildren and our relationship is very precious. We worked together as a couple to parent together and to build security into their lives. Initially, my husband took the lead and I supported him so that we were 'singing from the same hymn sheet' as it were, over time we increasingly developed 'our' way of operating and not just what he had done previously, and it was much more shared – otherwise it would have been unsustainable to live as a family where I was not sharing the discipline. We have been married for 36 years now. God was (and is) faithful and did an amazing work with us and we 'fast tracked' both marriage and parenting all in one go!"

Remember, it's about the children, but it's also about your relationship.

Sozo Stop!

Jesus, is there anything I need to forgive my parents for from my childhood?

_____

_____

_____

_____

I choose to forgive _____ for _____ (be specific and do it as much as you need to)

Jesus, what has the effect been on my life of my childhood experiences?

_____

_____

_____

Jesus, how do you want me to change the way I see my childhood?

_____

_____

_____

Jesus, how will this affect the way I parent my own children (or step children)?

If you have stepchildren, is there anything you need to forgive your stepchildren for?

Jesus, are there any ways I have blamed my stepchildren (to be) for struggles in our relationships?

Jesus, what's the truth about how you see our relationships?

The Sex Talk

One of the questions I (Darrell) sometimes ask the men I'm ministering to during a Sozo session is whether their Dad ever told them about women and sex, and I've never yet had someone tell me that they did. It's a question that usually arises because the person is carrying a lifetime of guilt and shame for the things they've looked at, thought about or done to the opposite sex. I am convinced this is something that could have been largely avoided if only Dad had plucked up the courage to talk about what has become for them a totally taboo and embarrassing topic. Perhaps slightly controversially it could be said that Dads have a similar responsibility to their daughters, honouring and loving them in the every day and modelling respect and admiration in a way that preps the daughter as to what to look for and expect from a man.

If you're planning on having children, a Dad will have three essential roles, to provide, to protect and to give identity. The first two of these are self-explanatory. The third needs to be clarified. Primarily it means that it's a Dad's job to help his children grow up to know who they are as (hopefully) Christians and (certainly) responsible members of society. Identity is knowing who and whose we are and what we stand for. Identity helps form character as a child grows up, it teaches the difference between right and wrong. Nowhere will this be more apparent than in their sexuality and how they approach the subject of sex. Please, as parents and especially as a Dad do not abdicate this important part of your role. Teach your children how to honour and respect the opposite sex, and explain the role of sex in adult married relationships.

We'd highly recommend the work that Kris Vallotten and Moral Revolution are doing in this whole area, see www.moralrevolution.com.

Postscript

Never underestimate the power of prayer. Prayer should run as a thread through your reading of this book. The Sozo Stops! will have brought you truths, the value of which typically far outweighs the fruit of the discussions arising from the Thought Stops! Bring everything to Him in prayer. Pray for your partner constantly, as they should for you. Pray for your children at all times. Start now. Prayer is outside of time… It is never too soon or too late to pray for what matters to you.

Never underestimate the value of other people's experience. There's rarely anything completely new in life so everything you're going through, all your questions, will have cropped up before. Know who to trust and be open with them. And just to clarify, your partner should be your best friend. In 20, 30 or more years' time it will be your friendship that keeps you together, so be open and vulnerable and may Father God, Holy Spirit and Jesus bless you both. And make it FUN!

Resources

You may find the following useful!

The 5 Love Languages by Dr. Gary Chapman

The Seven Principles for Making Marriage Work by John Gottman

The Science of Trust by John Gottman

Keep Your Love On! by Danny Silk

Boundaries by Cloud and Townsend

Love is a Choice: The definitive book on letting go of unhealthy relationships by Robert Hemfelt, Frank Minirth and Dr Paul Meier

Money and the Prosperous Soul by Stephen de Silva

The Act of Marriage: the beauty of sexual love by Tim and Beverly LaHaye

The Sozo for Couples Manual by Cocup and Gregg

To book a Sozo for Couples pre-marriage session visit www.sozoforcouples.org

Printed in Poland
by Amazon Fulfillment
Poland Sp. z o.o., Wrocław